The Game:

A Return to the Elan School

By Wayne Kernochan

~This book is dedicated to all survivors~

I

The computer has a history more than 2,000 years older than the internet, I know because I read about it on the internet. And though it's not my nature to trust something that tells its own history, what drew me to the World Wide Web in 2001 was that it told both sides. I was onto a story and had been offered a payment arrangement by Gateway, so I bought a computer.

I heard about Michael Skakel's murder trial like everyone else—on the television. Mike was a Kennedy cousin, suspected of killing his next door neighbor, Martha Moxley, in 1975. I remembered the story because I was in the residential treatment program he was sent to shortly after the murder.

The newspapers and television shows said he had admitted to killing Martha Moxley when he was a resident of the Elan school, but I knew the truth. He had, in fact said that he was the one who did it, but that confession was beaten out of him. The Elan school beat false confessions out of us as a way of breaking our spirit, but the news wasn't talking about that. They were, however, talking about the abuse at Elan. That was the story that needed to be told, and I had a plan to tell it.

My wife, Liz, found an in-depth story on a website. "Here you go." She looked at me. "You were in that place?"

I nodded.

She stood up. "Wow." She kissed my cheek. "I'm sorry you had to go through that."

"I've been through worse."

"It sounds pretty bad."

"It was an insane asylum, without the asylum." I sat and pointed to the computer screen. "This doesn't tell half of the story."

The news called the violence of the boxing ring, "physically rough treatment," and left many readers to believe we were subjected to questionable corporal punishment, but what we went through was torture and abuse. While some Elan people told the truth about what happened, some played it down and claimed the others were disgruntled losers with an axe to grind.

My story wasn't unique, but I knew it wasn't so much the story, as how it was told, or when. Timing is everything. Liz was against my plan from the beginning because I was going to testify against Mike.

"Are you crazy? The Kennedys will have you killed."

"I'm not going to hurt Mike. I'm going to help him."

"How?"

If I told her, it would have started a fight, so I lied. "I'm not sure yet."

"Well, you better be careful messing around with people like that."

They didn't scare me as much as the investigator in the case, Frank Garr. Cops made me more nervous than crooks, and narcotics cops in particular. It's an area of law enforcement that employed the worst of the worst. It was a dirty business, and they fought fire with fire, so though it wasn't a drug case, Frank was a drug cop and needed to be respected.

"So?" Liz wanted me to say something reassuring.

"So, what?" I said. "I'm not going to get myself killed over some rich douchebag I knew twenty five years ago."

She didn't seem convinced, but let it go.

#

The state of Connecticut didn't let the truth mess up their case against Michael Skakel. Almost every investigator who looked at the evidence believed his brother, Tommy, was the one who killed Martha Moxley. He failed a lie detector test and had changed his story. That was also the rumor when we were in Elan in 1978.

The public wanted to hang a Kennedy, and the media did their best to fan the flames. The newspapers published a picture of Mike wearing an ascot, with a smile on his face. "Who doesn't want to nail this guy?" I said to Liz. "He looks like a pretentious ass."

It's said that behind every great fortune is a great crime, and more times than not, one of those crimes is murder. The Kennedy family earned that reputation. There were theories that JFK had something to do with the death of Marilyn Monroe, and Teddy Kennedy was accused of letting Mary Joe Kopechne die when their car drove into the water in Chappaquiddick. It looked like Michael Skakel was going to pay for the sins of the family's past.

The state had two main witnesses, and one—Greg Coleman—had admitted to being high on heroin when he testified before the grand jury, so the state was hinging a murder case on John Higgins and his statement that Mike had confessed to him one night at Elan. Outsiders believed him, but anyone who went to Elan knew that if Mike had told John he killed someone and was going to get away with it, John would have gone straight to staff.

#

The Elan school started out as a drug program which used therapy based on aggressive group confrontation, started by an ex drug addict named, Charles E. Dederich, who broke away from Alcoholics Anonymous over the disdain shown for addicts in meetings. Synanon came along at a time when heroin addiction was panicking the masses, so when Hollywood took a liking to Chuck Dederich after his arrest for practicing medicine without a license, they made him a pop culture hero. Tough love therapy swept the country.

Similar programs sprung up from the popularity of the hardnosed treatment Synanon practiced. Drug addicts from all over the country joined Synanon, and members began to use what they called, "The Game," on them. Soon they were using it on kids and the results were remarkable, so Synanon's fame grew

Eventually, egotism stepped in. Synanon became a cult, and their god was Charles Dederich. Elan made its roots in the physically rough treatment, and took it to a level no one would believe until Michael Skakel was indicted for murder.

We didn't fight back in the boxing ring, as the media made it sound. If we did, it would go on until we were unable to. We covered up and let our opponents beat us as hard as they could. It took days or weeks to recover.

The media also didn't explain the spankings. People assumed we got our asses beat real good, but we were beaten bloody with paddles that had holes drilled in them to draw our blood. It also wasn't reserved for our asses. Many wore black and blue marks from the back of the neck to their ankles. I had seen kids get hundreds of whacks, and had gotten my share.

"I'm going to write a book." I announced.

"About Elan?" Liz said.

"No. About this bullshit trial.""

"If you're going to write a book, don't waste your time with this. Elan is the real story."

The murder trial would bring an audience. Once I had people's attention, the opportunity to tell the Elan story was there, but without the Kennedy name no one was interested. My plan was going to get their attention.

I found Martha Moxley's brother online, and called. "Hello."

"Is this John Moxley?" I said. "Are you the brother of Martha Moxley?"

He was guarded at first, which was understandable, so I got to the point quickly. He listened as I told him that I was in Elan with Michael Skakel, and had heard him admit that he killed Martha. When I was done he told me that I needed to speak to the prosecutor, Jonathan Benedict, or the state's investigator, Frank Garr.

"Give them my phone number. I'd be happy to speak to them."

The internet gave me everything I needed to know about Frank Garr and Jonathan Benedict. I hoped to speak to Frank first, who I believed was easier to deal with. I had spent my life around drugs and cops, not prosecutors, so it seemed more comfortable.

#

After ten years in twelve step programs I had two years twice, one year twice, and ninety days more times than I could remember. They talked about relapse not being a requirement, but for me it was constant. Sobriety was worse on me than drinking, so I sought relief in cocaine and alcohol.

The first side effect of sobriety is agoraphobia. Everyone gets it to some degree, and some are worse than others, but mine was worse than all of them. When the plug was in the jug, I broke down and couldn't leave the house. What I needed was someone to kick my ass to meetings, and that person was Paul V.

Paul didn't take, 'no,' for an answer. As painful and disturbing as leaving the house was, I knew what I needed, asked him to be my sponsor, and stayed clean and sober. All things being relevant, days seemed like weeks, so when asked how long I had been sober, I said, "A long time."

Paul had been following the Michael Skakel story. "No shit, you were there with this guy?"

"Yeah. The place was a nuthouse." I followed with a half dozen Elan stories, as Paul shook his head , and said, "Really?" or, "Jesus Christ," and other exclamations of horror. It was the first time I had spoken about Elan to anyone other than former residents in prison and drug programs.

"You were just a kid." Paul said. "What the fuck…" He couldn't think of anything to say, so he hugged me hard. "C'mon. The meeting is about to start."

#

After the meeting Paul wanted me to go for coffee, but I wanted to go home, so I made an excuse, but he insisted. "Fuck that, I want to hear more about that drug program."

Most people wanted to hear about Michael Skakel, but there were a good percentage interested in Elan. When I told them that the confession had been beaten out of Mike, and that I had no idea who killed Martha Moxley, and that the Michael I knew wasn't the killing type, most seemed disappointed. Paul asked who did kill her.

"The only real suspect up until Frank Garr looked at this was his brother Tommy." I sipped my coffee. "Every original investigator still thinks it's him." I shrugged. "I think they were trying to scare Mike into ratting on him, and it went awry."

"Huh?"

"I think they were trying to pressure him by building a half assed case against him and threatening to prosecute him…When the media caught the story, they ran with it."

Paul agreed with my assessment, and we spent hours talking about it over the next few days, and the story spread to three different fellowships. The trial was gaining celebrity type status, and people were paying attention.

\#

Liz became concerned. "Who is this narcotics cop you were talking to Paul about?"

Liz was home when Paul called, and was afraid the state of Connecticut was going to give me a hard time. I told her that I had a good feeling with Frank, and that he was just a means to an end. "Benedict is the guy I need to fear. Frank is a stepping stone."

"Why don't you leave these people alone?"

"I wish I could, but in order to tell the Elan story I need to do this."

There was no audience to sell a book to for decades because no one believed the insane nature of the abuse. That changed when the media told the stories. In spite of the new audience, it was still a longshot to sell the story to a publisher because Elan's lawyers were fierce. Joe Ricci harassed and threatened anyone who tried to tell the truth about what happened there.

Liz fought with me some more, but I stood my ground and assured her that I knew what I was doing. I ended the fight by saying, "I don't care what happens to me. I'm gonna get these fuckers for what they did to us." She didn't respond. "And I'm going to get them for what they did to Mary Jones."

\#

Frank Garr looked like a cop. We met at a Starbucks on Eighth Avenue, and when he walked in, everyone immediately knew. He wore the look well—he was in charge, and you were supposed to know it and conform. I did for the purpose of getting what I wanted.

I knew before we sat what he was going to ask first. "Do you mind if I record this conversation?" He took out a recorder.

"No, not at all."

He fumbled with the recorder, and then asked me to tell my story. I started by telling him that my memories of Elan were fuzzy, and my brain was worn from years of alcohol and drugs. When I told him that I was sober in AA he seemed impressed.

"What I remember, which I didn't see in the news, was the part about the golf club." I said. "I remember Mike saying it broke."

"He stabbed her with it?"

"Yes."

I told Frank that Mike was the night man at my house in Elan, and I was being tortured by staff into admitting that I was gay, and Mike told me that everyone admits to things that aren't true. I said that Mike told me about his admission to killing Martha, but didn't tell him that Mike said it was a false confession. Frank wouldn't put me on the stand if I did.

Liz and I discussed it before I left the house. "It's called lies of omission." She said.

"But there are no lies of omission laws. Nothing I'm saying is a lie."

"They'll get you for this."

The next question from Frank was, "Will you take a lie detector test?"

A quick search of the internet had given me everything I needed to know about lie detectors, and the most important thing wasn't passing or failing, but how you answer the question. "Sure, but that's not what I'm worried about. I'm more interested in you keeping me safe from the Kennedy family."

"They're not so scary."

"Uh-huh. Too many people end up dead around them."

He nodded.

Frank led my story in his direction, and we agreed that I needed to speak to the prosecutor, Jonathan Benedict. He asked if I would be willing to testify and I said, "Yes," which was good news. I had my foot in the door. What I left out was going to piss people off when I said it on the stand, and it was going to cause a stir, but I had to get past the State's Attorney, Jon Benedict first.

"You're also going to have to meet with the defense lawyer, Mickey Sherman."

"I have to meet with Mike's lawyer?"

"Sure. He has the right to confront all witnesses in the case."

"Then I need to tell you that these people may well dig up some shit from my past."

"Drugs?"

I nodded. "A lot of drunk and disorderly, and such, but that's all ancient history. I've been sober in AA for a long time."

We spent the next ten minutes discussing sobriety, AA and my history in the program. I told him that I was seven months sober, and left out the cocaine part of my relapses, so Frank found me to be a good witness. But there was one unasked question. The reward?

"I don't want any part of that. It's blood money."

He looked convinced. "Let's get you in to see Jonathan Benedict."

"Sounds good."

#

Outside, with the recorder turned off, I said, "Y'know, Coleman's testimony is shit now. Why should he get half the money, and not me?"

Frank stopped, and then told me not to mention the reward because people would think I was testifying merely for the money. "So far, that's been the norm: to accuse the witness of making their story up for the reward."

"I'm not worried about that. Like I said, go ahead and give me a lie detector test." I looked south, in the direction of my apartment. "People will just accuse me of doing it to get in front of a TV camera."

"I can get you ten thousand dollars."

"From who?"

"Don't worry about that. If Jonathan likes you and uses you on the stand I can get you ten grand."

"Done."

Frank left me there at the sidewalk, on Eighteenth Street and Eighth Avenue. When his cab was beyond sight I walked back into Starbucks, bought a coffee and sat at a booth, where I took the recorder off my hip and pulled the headphone cord out. It looked like a Walkman to the casual observer, but nothing was as it seemed.

Frank Garr wasn't the only one taping conversations.

II

A long time ago, in a faraway place called, Poland Springs, Maine, there was a great crime. Someone took something with promise and hope for millions of people, and turned it into a nightmare. I had heard about programs around the country that used the same therapy Synanon did, so I understood what Elan was supposed to be doing, but what they did with it was too bizarre to be believed. My mother had told me that Elan closed after a riot, so until Michael Skakel was put on trial it was a bad memory for me.

The Elan School was originally the Elan One Corporation, and we rarely had school. It was founded by a Harvard professor named Doctor Gerald Davidson, and a drug addict graduate of Daytop named Joe Ricci. When Joe Ricci died, my response was joy. Guilt followed, but was easily resolved because Joe Ricci was a monster who destroyed untold lives and caused innocent children to die.

On the bus to meet with Mickey Sherman, the memory of Joe led to memories of Elan, so though my brain kept telling me to ditch the whole thing and go home, I didn't. Another immediate side-effect of sobriety is fear, and mine was bad, but when the Elan memories rushed through my head, I became angry. I was in an Elan mind, and even fear couldn't mess with that.

The hotel bar was busy, and the crowd was wealthy. The Armani suits and Rolex watches were real. When the man at the desk heard who I was waiting for, I got the VIP treatment and was escorted to the bar. As I was about to order, a hush came over the crowd and Mickey Sherman made his entrance. It was planned and clumsily executed, but the crowd didn't notice.

He was buffed and polished, and looked like a game show host. Looks are deceiving. He was sharp, and he was mean. I read up on him. He didn't impress me because I was in my Elan mind. I was ready for him.

"Would you like a drink?"

"I don't drink. Thank you."

He seemed impressed, but it was hard to tell.

He pointed to a man he exchanged words with on his way in. "I have to talk to someone, but I'll be right back."

Everyone watched him, and then checked me out, then him again. Some continued to stare at me, but most were in awe of Mickey Sherman. I had him pegged right. He was making himself into a celebrity, and was hoping to use it to get Mike off. Executed correctly, it would be brilliant, but I had my doubts it would work. The media was too slanted against Mike.

When he got back we agreed to go to his room, where I agreed to let him tape the conversation, and told my story. I included the information I had left out when I spoke to Frank Garr. I told him that the confession was beaten out of Mike, and expected him to be happy, but he lost interest and said that Mike had never admitted to anything. I was of no use to him, so I asked for his help.

#

I told Paul about my plan to tank the prosecution during cross examination. An internet site said the maximum penalty for perjury in Connecticut was eighteen months. " Mickey Sherman told me I could get twenty years for perjury, so it's my old plan."

"Are you fucking crazy? These are some pretty serious people."

"I know. What I don't know is what to do."

"You better get out of this and keep your mouth shut."

I left Mickey Sherman's room with a lawyer, and told Frank that I wanted to drop the whole thing, and to speak to him, which he ignored. But when he asked to meet, and my lawyer approved it, I agreed. Before I hung up, I played part of the tape over the phone. When he realized it was the conversation we had outside Starbucks, he yelled. "What the fuck is this?"

"It's a shakedown Frank." I mustered up every bit of nerve I had. "I want the ten grand Frank. I don't want to testify."

"Why don't you speak to Jon Benedict, and then we'll talk."

"Don't fuck with me Frank. Or, I'll go to the highest bidder."

He hung up.

#

Jonathan Benedict was less than I expected. The way people spoke about him painted the picture of a strong personality, but his wasn't. The awe he was being shown was because it was his show, and his decision who went in front of the cameras.

Frank Garr and Mickey Sherman were dancing for the crowds. Jonathan Benedict was on a different level. From the slant in the media, it was obvious he was dancing behind the scenes. And, he was real good at it.

Before I left the house, Liz asked, "What are you going to tell this man?"

"Something no one wants to hear. The truth."

Jonathan Benedict was nice, but saw I was of no value as a hostile witness. He had researched and interviewed enough Elan survivors to know I was trouble, so he gave me a check for seventy five dollars and sent me on my way. I met Frank in the hallway, on the way out.

"I still want the money."

"Fuck you, ya get nothing from me."

He told me that he knew Mickey Sherman his whole life, and was sure he didn't want the tape, so I told him I would give it away to the media if it was worthless. He offered me seventy five hundred dollars.

I nodded.

"I'll call you."

"Okay."

#

Four days later, the phone rang. "Hello."

"You're in big trouble, Wayne."

"Who is this?"

""I'm the wind, and you don't want me blowing down Sixteenth Street…Greg Coleman's death wasn't an accident."

Greg Coleman had just died of a heroin overdose. "How hard would it be for Frank to have someone give him a hot shot?" I asked Liz.

"I told you, you were going to get us killed."

The voice of the man on the phone was the voice of a killer. I know because I know killers. So as they tried and convicted Michael Skakel of murder, and everyone played their roles, I drank. I was the same piece of shit coward, sober as drunk, without the booze to kill the pain, so I took my medicine and waited to die, and forgot about Elan.

I took a liking to the computer and the internet. It became an obsession, and a good friend. People in chat rooms liked me and were happy when I signed on. Message boards and instant messaging drew me deeper into the obsession.

I stopped following Elan news and rarely checked on Mike. Life took me in other directions and the internet was big enough to avoid Elan and its people. But one day, seven years later, my good friend the computer turned on me and let a monster back in my life.

III

Monsters are real; I know because I see them and remember their faces for when I see them again. The world inside the internet had its fair share, but was generally a friendly place. However, on December 8th, 2009 it let the worst of the worst back into my life. A thirty year old nightmare from Poland Springs, Maine.

"Danny, Fucking, Bennison."

"What?" Liz got up.

"Danny Bennison." I pointed to the computer screen. "He's on an Elan survivor group acting like a survivor."

"That horrible guy?"

"That's the one."

He was nervous, I could see. His banter was friendly and reassuring, but his criticism of Elan felt hollow and forced. In a discussion about abuse, Danny wrote comforting words but they made me apprehensive, so I wrote to the site administrator.

"Hey, you have Danny Bennison as a member. He was my director. What's his story?"

She responded by telling me that he was a liar and told me to expose him to the group, but I wrote back and said we should wait and watch, because he was one of the worst, and that he drilled holes in the paddle to draw blood during spankings. I told her that Danny was the director who tied Mary Jones to the back of his car and dragged her around the grounds.

\#

"He avoids the subject of being staff." Liz said. She pointed to a comment. "But his story sounds pretty bad." I looked over her shoulder. "He went through that place too, ya know?"

I knew that and considered it, but was being wary. "I'm going to be careful with this guy."

18

The next morning, I checked the group, and the administrator had exposed Danny without asking or alerting me, and Danny went on the warpath. I couldn't read it, so I posted that I understood Elan damaged us all, forgave him, and left the group.

#

Fear is easy if you can recognize it and use it to your advantage. You never master fear, but you live longer if you understand it. You can dance with it, but you can never lead. Fear is absolute, I know because I've had monsters in my life.

"He used to lower his voice, real guttural, and drag the words out, like Marty Kruglik used to do." I said. I mimicked him.

Liz grimaced. "Who is Marty Kruglick?"

"A child abuser." I said. "A sick, depraved child abuser…He bought the program hook line and sinker." I sat and refreshed the computer. "That's why I'm not buying Danny's bullshit. He was the same way."

#

I had five different memoirs in ten different folders, and one agented out. The first didn't sell, but I was back in the game with the second. Plus, I had the Elan story going. Things were good, but the Elan book was taking an emotional toll. When Danny became real, the fear came back, and fear wasn't always easy for me. I eventually recognized him as no threat, and stayed away from Elan groups online.

I came upon Danny again on Facebook, in a discussion about Michael Skakel. He was being abusive, stating his opinion as a good enough reason to throw a man in prison for life, so I confronted him about his past as the assistant resident director at my house in Elan, and he threatened to come to my house.

"Are you threatening me Dan? I'm not a scared 14 year old kid anymore."

He threatened to sue me, then left the conversation, and deleted his posts, so I did the same and forgot about him until I found the conversation copied and pasted, and brought to a discussion on a website called, Fornits.

I had told Danny that I wrote a book about him and Elan, and that it was cut out of an earlier version of the book I had subbed out by my agent, and he and his friends laughed, and said no publisher was ever going to fight with Élan's lawyers. I agreed and decided to self-publish.

\#

"I'm going to finish the Elan book." I said to Liz.

"The Elan book is 'the' book. I've been saying that for years."

She enjoyed being right.

"The problem is getting going."

"Then, get going."

We agreed when I wrote my memoirs that the Elan book, though the beginning of the story, would be the last book. It was better to tell my secrets before telling theirs because if they had anything damaging on me, they would use it.

When I fell on the ice in front of our cabin in Patterson, New York, in 2008, my feet came out from under me, and I landed on my neck, so my first thought was to move my arms and legs. They were fine. The next thought was of my back, and that was not.

The pain was bad enough that I knew I was never going to work again. Even if someone paid for rehabilitation and surgery, I was never going to be physically able. My life was over, and we were going to lose everything. Our run of bad luck had come to the end, and my spirit was broken.

Liz saw what happened through the living room window and came. "Are you okay?"

I couldn't respond and felt a strange warmth come over me. The pain went away, and calm came over me. It was a sense of security, like it felt as a child under the covers. I didn't try to speak because words were meaningless. My first thought was of suicide, and wasn't accompanied by anxiety or fear, but acceptance. I knew then, that it was right.

Liz helped me to the couch, found a heating pad and applied it to my shoulder, which helped. There was no position that was comfortable, so I shifted a lot. We opted to tape the heating pad to my back. "I need to sit at the computer anyway."

Once mobile, I began a suicide note which started, "Fuck you all," and went into an angry rant for five pages. When I ran out of steam, I had tea, then sat and read what I had written. Aside from a few spelling errors it was pretty good, so I continued with an acknowledgement of the things I had done wrong. By page fifty it began to look like an AA ninth step, and by page seventy five it began to read like a book

I was determined to die and no one was going to read what I wrote until I was gone, so I didn't care, and with that freedom, the truth came out for the first time. When the truth came out, I wrote for weeks. When the manuscript hit 300 pages, I found an agent and editor, and the book became a reason to live.

The consensus after a few weeks with an agent was that the writing needed work. "It's good, but it's all over the place at times." Liz said.

"What should I do?"

"Study writing…Join a writer's group."

#

Bad luck followed us from Patterson to Philadelphia, and then to Connecticut. It got worse when we moved to New York. The only things that went right were related to my books. When rejections came, I dealt with them well, but I had great successes as a new writer. I had signed with two agents in eleven months. Aside from money it was a good year. Then, I ran into him again.

"Danny Bennison."

"Again?" Liz shrugged. "I told you to block him and stay away from him."

"He's talking shit about me on Fornits again."

"Don't..."

"I'm not..."

A book page on Facebook was intended for cult or classic books, but there were no rules that said it had to be. I started one for, A Life Gone Awry: My Story of the Elan School, and posted the first chapter in the discussion forum.

And it began.

#

In the first week, A Life Gone Awry was joined by over one hundred people and had over five thousand views. The best part was that Elan survivors didn't know yet. The attention was from my writer friends and family.

Liz and I watched the views as they went up and down, and couldn't find a pattern. "Figure out what you're doing to make them go down, and change it." She said.

Week two I found the pattern. "It's not something I'm doing wrong; it's something I'm doing right."

"Huh?

I showed her the graphs. "It's not what I'm doing to make views go down. It's what I'm doing to make them go up." I pointed to the dates that were spiked. "The views go up every time I post a chapter."

"That's great."

"It would be, if I had more chapters to post."

"Oh."

I stood. "Yeah, this started off as a work in progress kind of thing, and now I have hundreds of people waiting for chapter nine. I barely edited the eight I posted."

She sat. "Then let me check my e-mails real quick. You need to get busy."

I wrote improvisational memoir for a waiting audience as the views and comments increased. Private messages came to me on three different social networks. From all indications, the book was a hit.

#

Mark Babitz was the first Elan survivor to find the book page. I had seen his name and read his posts on Elan groups, and knew we were on the same side. He had a special hatred for Marty Kruglick; He introduced himself by asking about Danny Bennison.

"Hi Wayne. Is this the same Danny B we have all grown to know and love on Fornits?"

We wrote back and forth for days. Mark told me Elan's dirty secrets, and Marty Kruglick stories. "His father was a famous psychiatrist. He developed the profile that caught the serial killer, Richard Speck."

"What about the rumor that Marty was in Elan for raping a kid, is that true?"

"The rumor is that it was the son of a gangster from New York. A real live Mafioso."

"That's fucked up."

"That's why he went in there at fourteen years old and never left. He's a lifer."

"He's guilty."

"I think so."

I told him that I had forgotten about Elan after my mother said it had been closed following a riot. The story made more sense than it was still in business. Until I found the Elan Survivor site I had no idea there was a campaign going on the internet to close them down.

Mark warned me about Elan people on the internet, and asked if he could post old articles about Elan on the book page, and I agreed. He finished. "I can't wait to see Danny's reaction."

"I can't wait to see Elan's reaction."

Sharon Terry inherited Elan when Joe Ricci died. Jeff Gottlieb, one of my directors, was still there. They still had their team of lawyers. I expected to hear from them as soon as I announced the book page to the Elan sites, which I did that night.

#

Views doubled in the first day and stayed that way for weeks. Private messages from Elan survivors poured in, and people began posting on the page. They commented about their time in Elan, and asked for more chapters as they read. I wrote and posted chapters, unedited, or with a rough read through. It wasn't perfect, but it was good enough for my readers.

Matt Hoffman was the second Elan survivor to contact me. I had sent him a private message months earlier explaining who Danny Bennison was, and asked him to keep it quiet. Then, I explained that I was writing a book about Elan. He kept my secret.

Matt's bane was Jeffrey Gottlieb. He told me his Jeff Gottlieb story. "They asked Jeff if he wasn't working at Elan, what would he be doing." Matt said. "And, Jeff stood there a long time, ya know, like he was in deep thought. He drags it out for like twenty minutes. Then, finally, he looks at the room, and says, "Sell shoes."

I laughed.

"But here's the worst part. Gottlieb isn't qualified to sell shoes."

I laughed harder.

"But he's torturing kids in Poland Springs." He said.

"It's just Poland now. They took off springs."

"I noticed that. Probably has something to do with water sales."

"I'm sure."

Matt told me about the days before I got there, which were of particular interest to me because people from the early 1970s claimed the insane violence began around 1975. Matt told horror stories of physical and mental abuse.

Electric sauce had been banned by 1978, but Matt experienced it. He told me they threw all the waste from the garbage cans and ashtrays into a soup, and poured it over people's head, and once they made a girl wear a crown of tampons dipped in catsup. "What's the therapeutic value in that?"

I didn't know what to say.

"The people who stayed there for many years, like, Jeff, Marty and Sharon, are serial child abusers, and should rot in jail."

I agreed.

"Have you heard anything from Danny?"

"Nary a word."

"He's hiding."

I checked the people who joined the book page every few hours, and was sure Danny would join eventually, but his sister joined first. She commented at the end of a chapter, and asked why I wouldn't change Danny's name, so I told her he was trolling a survivor site.

She said, "He has a family, you know?"

I wrote. "I believe people in a survivor group have the right to know who's holding their hand."

She didn't respond, but Danny joined the group that night. I deleted and blocked him when a friend asked me why Danny was sending her private messages. She wasn't the only person to ask about him. Four women complained to me that he was being abusive to them.

Danny dropped off the internet radar other than the people he contacted privately. There were no flame wars on the page site. I was told that was a miracle because all Elan discussions and groups end badly. I hadn't had one negative post. Not even by Danny.

#

In the beginning of February I found a discussion on the Elan Alum site in which a poster accused everyone who left Elan and said nothing, of being complicit in their crimes against children. I was guilty, and knew he was right. I was so happy to get out of there in 1980 that I didn't look back.

"I didn't think about Elan, except when I ran into someone in prison, or the nut house."

Liz laughed because she thought I was kidding, but the prison was full of them, and the state hospital had a fair share. I ran into others in the streets and AA. Elan survivors crashed and burned after graduation. There were those who did well, but they were the exception.

My life was falling apart financially, so we had just taken the train to Connecticut to borrow money from my sister, and found my nephews and their friends reading the book. I had been debating leaving the sexual abuse in, but Danny was an internet joke so I wanted to take it out. Seeing them reading the book settled the debate.

#

Some nightmares never end. When you wake, they're not over. They're paused, or changed. Then, they're replayed, and played again. If your nightmares are like mine you've been having the same one your entire life.

Some aspects of nightmares disappear for long periods of time, like Elan did, but you realize after a while that nothing ever went away. When you've had as many nightmares as me it's easy to see where they bled into other things in other dreams.

When the immediate shock of meeting Danny Bennison wore off, I was left with the reality that Elan wasn't gone from my head, even after thirty one years. It wasn't uncommon. The e-mails and private messages I received from fellow survivors made that clear. Survivors of other programs had the same nightmares. I got a message about Straight Inc.

"What's Straight Inc.?"

She told me that Straight Inc. spawned from the Seed, which was a spinoff from the mother program, Synanon. She recounted abuse similar to Elan, and said Straight had been closed down by lawsuits and investigations.

"I thought Elan was closed for a long time. My mom told me."

"Well, Straight didn't stay closed." She told me the owners had changed the name, and moved, but advocates followed them and protested, and closed them down again. "They just keep popping up."

"Money grubbing freaks."

"They killed my brother."

"I'm so sorry."

She was quiet for a while, but wrote back that night to say that her reason for contacting me was to let me know that she had created a website for A Life Gone Awry, and paid the bill. It was her contribution. I thanked her repeatedly, but with all the grace I could muster it didn't express how much it meant to me.

"While I have an audience, I want to hang all these motherfuckers. Who ran Straight?"

"Mel Sembler. Miller Newton started KIDS of New Jersey."

"Another?"

"Yeah. There were lots of them."

The guilt of having left and been quiet about Elan was nagging at me. Until the trial of Michael Skakel I was silent out of fear for Joe Ricci and his lawyers. Both were bad situations. But, when Joe died there was no reason not to keep trying. I also had no fear from the threatening phone caller anymore. I lost interest because there was no market for the book.

The phone rang. "Hello."

"Wayne, it's Mark."

"Hey bro, what's up?"

"Are you online?"

"I was just about to sign off."

"Check out the Lewiston Sun Journal website. They left you a birthday present on the front page."

I entered the name into search and hit, send, and the page loaded. The home page gave a list of sites with related articles about the Sun Journal. I found the correct link and clicked on it.

"Holy shit."

"Yeah." He said. "Holy shit."

The headline read:

"Elan School closing after Web campaign to close it down."

"Happy birthday to me."

IV

On March 23rd, 2011 the Elan school announced they were going out of business, and the news went viral on the internet. Within hours there were events, parties and active discussions on message boards and blogs. Most survivors were happy and celebrated the announcement. There were some who weren't as happy, and the arguments began.

The two arguments from pro-Elan people were, "Why don't you get over it already?" and, "Elan changed," and sometimes we bothered to answer the questions, but were met with abusive language from people who became abusers when they were in Elan. Most were old-timers who justified their abuse by convincing themselves that they were helping people, but among the more recent residents there were two sides, one of which was saying Elan saved their lives.

Matt said, "Elan was one year into a softer hands approach after abusing children for forty years. This wasn't something recent. The internet campaign against Elan has been going on for ten years."

"So, their reputation finally caught up to them?"

"Big time."

From what the older anti-Elan people were saying it was clear that was what had happened. The campaign against Elan began after the Michael Skakel trial, and the information became overwhelming after ten years of advocates posting Elan's atrocities online. People who checked into them were shown the truth, and chose not to send their kids there. Declining enrollment was caused by due diligence on the part of parents and advocates.

In the three months prior to closing their doors, Elan hadn't commented on A Life Gone Awry. Jeff Wimbelton told me that their silence was louder than any protest they may have made. "They couldn't defend themselves against it. Even pro-Elan people haven't attacked it."

"I wish I felt like it had something to do with them closing."

29

"You don't understand." Matt said. "We' got the ball over the plate. Your book hit it out of the park."

"I wish I believed that."

"Well, believe it."

#

That night Matt, Mark and I talked in an Elan Facebook group all night. We posted until the sun came up, over eight hundred replies. Like old friends, years after the war, we told our stories, and spoke about friends who had passed away or had disappeared into the abyss Elan created.

Mark said he had gotten his records, so I asked about mine. "Those are probably long gone." He said. "They don't want a trail leading back to those days."

Matt agreed. "They said there was a fire, and the records from our days were burned up."

I had heard that story. "I was an expeditor for two months, and I turned in hundreds of papers a week. You're talking about hundreds of thousands of documents. The house would have burned to the ground."

"That's for sure." Matt said.

"Was there an insurance claim? A nine one one call maybe?"

"That's a good question."

Mark was our resident information man. He could find almost anything on the internet. He said he couldn't find anything about a fire in the 1980s. "Unless, maybe there was no claim."

"Joe set fires for insurance. Do you really think he wouldn't make a claim the one time there was a real fire?" I asked.

Matt said that Joe Ricci had set the fire at Scarborough Downs that killed eleven horses. "Now, Sharon's going to open a casino, and call it Racino and more blood money for her."

"That's fucked up."

We bid each other goodnight at eight o'clock in the morning, Eastern Standard Time, and Matt and Mark's worst demon was gone from the world. Elan wasn't the only one for me. It wasn't the worst either. The next day Danny went on an internet rampage, and my book was the theme.

#

What do you do when your monster has become a hapless fool? Danny Bennison's posts about me and my book were abusive, vulgar, threatening and riddled with bad spelling. People told me he was drinking, and that was his drunken persona. It was pathetic.

"You can't win." Liz said. "Block him and ignore him or you'll look like the bully."

"Too late. I've already slayed him."

It was too easy, and the anger and fear I felt for so long allowed me to justify it, but I knew it was wrong, and not only wrong, but wrong that I enjoyed it. Is it any different if the person you're abusing is an abuser?

We didn't always hate being forced to abuse each other in Elan. Often, by the time the person who was being punished was in the position to be abused, we had been tortured by their actions, and went into the ring eager to beat them. The online abuse had a familiar feel.

Liz sighed. "Turn off the computer and get away from all of that Elan drama, or it's going to make you crazy."

I laughed. "Too late."

"I'm not kidding. You're already on the internet for days at a time."

Not only that, but when I did log off I couldn't sleep. Though insomnia was once gone from my life, the Elan drama kicked it back up. I had been awake for days at a time for months since Danny reentered my life.

"I have to deal with him when he gets dirty, and he's good at it. I just got a private message that he joined my writers group."

"Did he?"

I pointed to the computer screen. "Check it out."

#

Jeff Wimbelton had sent me a list of groups Danny had joined. "He's watching you, but I'm watching him."

"What should I do?"

"If you mention him, he'll reveal himself."

I posted a thread titled, "A sparkling review from a man who wants to kill me," and posted Danny Bennison's manifesto, in which he praised my writing, and then went on to call me a liar. Then, I posted Danny's other manifesto. It was a fake, I knew because I had read all of Danny's posts on Fornits, and parts were cherry picked from them, but it was also completely in context, and showed Danny's true internet persona as a predator and abuser.

Danny admitted that the first manifesto was his, and then denied writing the second, which was fine with me because in the first he claimed as staff he saw three current staff members abuse children. His exact words were, "I watched Staff and Directors leave en-mass and I watched 3 people who are still there deny they are doing children harm, It is beyond shameful."

The moderator banned Danny, and the Elan people had fun with him for being spanked by a bunch of writers, and I moved on to Topix, where he was attacking me on another discussion. Then, Facebook, and so on. It never ended. Danny found new venues every time he was banned from one.

"He'll move on to the next group and abuse people there." Matt said. "He hasn't changed one bit since he was staff."

Mark posted the writers group's best response on Facebook:

"Danny, are you a writer? Or are you just stalking Wayne across the internet trying to refute what he says in his book? Because quite frankly, this is a site for WRITERS, not flame wars.

Wayne doesn't promote his book here. For one, 'promotion' doesn't really apply to free books. Second, this site isn't about book promotion. Wayne has, however, discussed his book here with his peers in the writing community, and his story was gripping enough to cause many of us to check into the history of Elan School and the charges against it.

Here's the major facts as they apply to this site:

1--If you're here to refute Wayne's book, you're here under false pretenses. You are a cyber-stalker, cluttering up a writer's forum with your own personal agenda.

2--No one here cares about who you are, what your history is, or what you did or did not do at Elan. No one here cares if you remember Wayne or not. His book is about what HE remembers from Elan, not you, and it is not his responsibility to compensate for your lack of memory regarding him.

3--It's not our responsibility to investigate the 'war of words' you're having with Wayne beyond what occurs on this site. And, quite frankly, I find it so utterly, horribly creepy that ANYONE would cyber-stalk a victim of abuse and challenge him to verify that abuse or corroborate it in some way that I can honestly say all you're doing is undermining yourself. This behavior is the behavior of an abuser, not a victim. So all you've accomplished with this at least as far as I'm concerned is to confirm everything that Wayne has said--a confirmation, I might add, that has been already provided by hundreds of other Elan victims across the internet.

I'd suggest that it is in your best interests to stop the stalking and just let it drop, Danny. You're not doing yourself any favors with this behavior. All you're doing, in fact, is making his case for him. I would assume that's not your intent?

Let it go. And leave the Elan controversy on the Elan sites, instead of dragging them onto writers' forums that aren't involved.

Best wishes for your future endeavors."

#

April 1st came to no hurrah. Elan people were uncharacteristically quiet. The last day of Elan's existence didn't even make the paper. "This feels like a cover-up."

"It is." Matt said. "Sharon has had that newspaper in her pocket for years, like so many politicians."

"It's amazing how well kept their secrets are."

"They spread a lot of money around in forty one years."

There was more than money at work hiding Elan's secrets. Without the Michael Skakel trial, most people would never have heard of it. Joe Ricci ran for governor, and attacked Angus King's wife and family, yet, King never used Elan and its reputation against him.

"Small town politics." Matt said.

"I think he was told the subject of Elan was off limits." I said. "Joe was an outsider. Mainers would have eaten his heart for attacking the guy's wife."

"I don't know what to think."

"I just think it's strange that even his enemies never used that reputation against him."

Matt insisted money was the cause, but I had read Danny's real manifesto closely, and in it he claimed that as staff, he witnessed residents coming in from mental institutions, including mentally ill and autistic children, and was convinced Elan was more than just a drug program to the state of Maine—it was a secret. What I couldn't figure out was how to prove it.

The people of the state of Maine hated Elan and the reputation it earned them, which was unfair because the state deceived them. They were told that the state did regular unannounced inspections, while Elan was getting a three day notice of any inspection. Ex director Ken Zaretsky said during an interview for Details Magazine, that as staff, "We lied through our teeth."

The state of Illinois spoke out against Elan and removed residents, and the state of New York did the same, but yet it continued. Even in its closing, you were hard pressed to get a bad word from anyone about Elan.

Mark told me, "It's eerie. Even Synanon was exposed and prosecuted."

"Were they?"

"Sure. In the late seventies the government took them to court to revoke their tax-free status, and they called this therapy brainwashing and torture."

"Where can I see this?"

"Paul Morantz has a blog. He's the guy Chuck Dederich tried to kill."

"Really?"

"Yup, they put a rattlesnake in his mailbox."

I followed the link Mark sent me to a blog that told the story of Chuck Dederich and Synanon and began to read the history of attack therapy. We called it Peer Pressure, and it was called other things, but Synanon called it, "The Game," and used threats, intimidation and murder to protect the program and its leader.

My education began.

#

According to Paul Morantz's blog profile, he was an attorney in Los Angeles who specialized in brainwashing cases and helped people who had been taken advantage of by religious and self-help cults. In 1988, in a case against the Unification church, he got the California Supreme Court to recognize brainwashing as a harmful act, and allow victims to sue for damages.

Chuck Dederich gave the order to kill Paul Morantz, which was carried out by his Imperial marines. They cut the rattle off a rattlesnake and put it in his mailbox. Morantz was bitten by the snake, but survived. Chuck Dederich and two of his followers were arrested.

Charles E. Dederich was called Chuck Dederich or CED. From the information I found, he was a disgruntled member of AA with a lot of influence among drug addicts and dual addicted members. His plan was to break away and create a similar program, where addicts weren't subjected to hate.

CED's plan went better than expected. Many heroin addicts put down the needle when they joined him. The program was spoken about, and referrals began, and CED was a local hero. Then he was arrested for practicing drug treatment without a license and the Game became a game because Hollywood defended him and Dederich became a celebrity.

In an AA chatroom, a member told me that the local authorities were bombarded by letters and phone calls attacking Dederich and his group because he was stealing members from AA—a plan that backfired on them.

"Alcoholics Anonymous is neck deep in this shit. Art Barker founded the Seed—he was an AA guru too." Jeff Wimbelton said.

"The Seed?"

"It was the beginning of Straight Inc."

"Art barker?" I said. "He sounds like a game show host."

"He was a comedian, and Jackie Gleason's sponsor."

"Then, he had his hands full."

He laughed. "He sure did."

#

Chuck Dederich's first arrest was the beginning of Synanon. Famous people expressed outrage that someone who was working miracles with drug addicts was being forced to stop, and convinced the masses to join them. The media caught the story and a movie was made about Synanon. CED became a pop culture icon. The people fell in love with Synanon.

There were dances and community outreach, and famous people joined them as non-drug users. Celebrities swarmed to the big events, and its popularity soared. Fame is power, and CED's power grew until he made the group into a church, and someone asked the question, "Who will be God?"

I called Mark Babitz. "Hell yeah, he was God. Dude went stone fucking crazy with power. He had an army…They had their own form of karate."

"Ben Parks said the people running the game were gamed themselves."

"You think the leaders were being played?"

"Sure, why not?"

"They all wanted to be God."

"This is incredible. I would write a book about this shit, but who would believe it?"

"That was their greatest weapon. The shit they did was so crazy that no one ever believed it." He said.

"Like Joe Ricci."

"Like Mel Sembler. Like Miller Newton. All of them."

After watching, "Surviving Straight Inc." the documentary about Mel Sembler's house of horrors, I was sure that brainwashing was being used as therapy, but we were children, which made it illegal. The governor of California changed the laws to allow older residents of Synanon to practice the game on new members, but it was agreed on for cocky young heroin addicts.

"Morantz would call Elan a brainwashing cult, and their treatment torture." Mark said. "Hell, Morantz was one of the government's expert witnesses against Synanon."

"Funny, Dederich didn't go to prison for attempted murder of a federal witness."

"That probably pissed Morantz off."

"Does he know about Elan?"

"I don't know."

"Because, while he was on the west coast calling this brainwashing and torture, they were on the east coast paying Elan and Straight to do it to us.."

\#

On Facebook, a friend and I were exchanging private messages about God, and forgiveness, and Danny Bennison. She entered the discussion on the book page when Danny's sister posted.

I hadn't been sleeping, was angry all the time and New York was expensive and crowded. Liz and I fought all the time, and I was looking for something better. Some program people called religion a cult, but my favorite years were the ones in which I believed in God. I wasn't into religion, but spirituality suited me just fine.

Cate Capozzi used to say, "God loves us best when we're broken."

I was broken when my friend stepped into that discussion because I was torn about whether Elan created people like Danny Bennison, or people like Danny Bennison created Elan. Matt and Mark agreed it was the latter. I wasn't sure.

\#

When the lights went dark on Elan, everyone went their own way, and though we retained the fellowship of that, we hated that we had it, and resented that the truth had never been told by anyone of importance. Straight Inc. had been closed down by lawsuits, and survivors had stood up and told their stories, but Elan survivors never got the opportunity. They closed during a bad economy because of declining enrollment, so Elan faded from the public eye, and so did we. I wasn't satisfied.

When the book didn't draw a lawsuit I began to attack the owner, Sharon Terry, on every Maine business, TV, Radio, and political Facebook page I could find, calling her a child abuser and explaining that her plan to open a casino was fine, just not with her in charge. She did nothing.

Matt called. "Maybe you should tell the story of Jimmy Shiplett or Phil Williams. That might get Sharon's attention."

"Who are they?"

"They were both killed at Elan."

"They died?"

"They were murdered."

Phil Williams was put in the boxing ring for insubordination. He was given an order, but complained of headaches and refused. They beat him in the head until he collapsed, then left him foaming at the mouth for an hour before calling an ambulance.

"The medical examiner called it an aneurism or something. Joe Ricci probably threatened him." Matt said. "Either that or someone else. Elan's influence and money are widespread."

#

When I hung up, Danny was on Facebook claiming his survivor status. The previous day a friend had told me that he was inclined to feel sympathy for Danny because of the endless attacks, so instead of fighting with him I apologized.

"Shame on me for making fun of your spelling. That was abusive. It was wrong." I wrote.

Danny went silent, but the next day sent me a private message and friend request. The monster was at the door asking to be let in, and I remembered the story of the snake that bit the man who nursed him to health and said, "You knew I was a snake when you took me in." I knew what I was getting into.

Danny didn't remember me. No one could be so brazen to someone they had sexually abused. I kept quiet about it because I didn't want him to remember. If he did, his power over me would be painful.

I read the private message, and again he said he tried and spent sleepless nights, but couldn't remember me. He went on to invite me to work with him to fight abusive programs. I friended him and let the monster in the door. At the same time I was on the phone with Matt.

"You friended Bennison? You better be careful. He's a snake."

"I know. I just want to see if there's anything good in that man before I drop the bomb on him."

"I can save you the trouble. There isn't."

I laughed. "You have a special hate for Danny, huh?"

Danny had threatened to come to Matt's house with some friends and brainwash Matt, and the way it was written was undoubtedly a threat. He had done it to me twice. He had also threatened a woman who had survived Straight Inc. on Fornits. Matt hated him.

"Bennison has staff syndrome. He still thinks that he gets to say something, and the subject is closed."

#

My writer friend had told me the story of a prisoner of war who forgave his captors, and had requested to meet the chief officer, his worst tormentor, but was turned down. "In the end he couldn't bring himself to meet his victim." She said.

"I fear that's going to be Danny's response."

"Hopefully not."

The next day, Danny blocked me on Facebook, and left a link to an AA blog, and an article titled: "Meet Diablo: aka Danny Bennison." The article started with Danny's threat to Matt, and told about me and my book. The writer asked how someone could be so horrible to someone that the person called him a monster thirty years later.

Danny went quiet.

#

I wasn't part of the anti-AA blog that wrote the article Danny linked me to. I had never heard of it. After investigating, it was obvious he was still abusive, threatening and a bully. I couldn't block him because he had me blocked. Matt told me that was one of his tricks.

"You're better off rid of him." Liz said. "Now, maybe you can get some writing done."

I hadn't written in months. "Sounds good."

I wanted to turn off the computer determined not to sign back on, but we had no TV or radio, so the internet was my only connection to the outside world. I didn't want to be away for long. What I needed to do differently is to share time between the internet and real life and find balance.

People criticize, and say the internet isn't real and the people are phony, but that isn't true. The internet is real, I know because I got lost in there.

V

The internet was interesting at first, quickly became an everyday thing, then an obsession. I had met real people, felt real feelings and been all over the world without leaving the house. I found love and support, and fear and loathing, all without getting out of my pajamas.

People on my writers group complained that the internet took too much of their time and had themselves temporarily banned to meet deadlines. Real life was getting bad, so I had done the opposite and retreated into chat rooms and message boards with my friends twenty four hours a day, as my insomnia was at its worst.

After ten years in AA the realization that I wasn't an alcoholic or drug addict hit me. It began with a song lyric in my head that lasted for over four months, which kept me awake for days at a time. When I was able to fall asleep I woke with lyrics in mid verse. I realized the power of Obsessive Compulsive Disorder when I planned to put a gun in my mouth. When my doctor explained what OCD was, it all made sense.

Cocaine—and crack in particular—was my drug of choice because it was perfect for an OCD. Nothing was more important than the next hit, including my inevitable death. "I think it kept me from killing myself for years."

"That's pretty perceptive." Liz said. "Why don't you include it in the new book?"

"I'm working on it."

"Good for you."

I had five books in seven folders, all different, but the same—undone. There were two memoirs started and set aside, but the story of the program and its history was the only one I could think about. The problem was that it required hundreds of hours of reading. I slept one or two hours a day, and was coming to grips with OCD, and used it to my advantage. Improvise, adapt, and overcome. When I was a cab driver I used insomnia bouts to drive twenty four or forty eight hours shifts, and make lots of money.

There was no crash from the insomnia bout after Elan closed. It continued because our living situation was terrible. We were living with my brother, who was deep into a crack addiction, so we stayed in our room with the door closed most of the time. But, he also drank too much, so he would get drunk and knock on our door to tell us about the niggers, the Jews, and the towelheads. He wasn't all there to begin with, but alcohol and drugs had left nothing good in his head.

The first of every month was a struggle to get him to pay the rent. It had fallen behind, and the fighting began. My brother has always been a bully, but I had never seen it directed at women. He screamed at Liz with his fists balled up, which ended up in a fist fight. My father got in-between us and ended up with a bloody nose.

"We're never going to be able to save money to get out of here." I told Liz. "We're stuck."

"I know."

"I told you this was going to get bad."

As much as I hated to remind her that I had told her so, it kept coming out because she was angry at me. I would have stayed where we were in Connecticut until we fixed our car or found something with better access to stores. Our situation there was tough, not impossible.

"We didn't have a car—"

I cut her off. "We were fine. You wanted to live in the big city and go to museums and libraries…But now we can't afford to get on the train to go to the food stamp office."

"That's his fault too." She pointed to my brother's bedroom door. "He won't let up as long as he thinks you have money."

"He's a crackhead."

"He's a predator."

He was both.

#

After walking away from twelve step programs, my friends didn't want to get together because I wasn't going to meetings. Even my family treated me as though it were just a phase I was going through, and relapse was just around the corner. Instead, I stayed clean and didn't think about getting high.

By the time we got to New York we were thousands of dollars in debt, which was getting harder to handle. There was less money and more people to pay, so we weren't popular. I made meals from scratch, made my own cigarettes and didn't have any other habits. I could exist on very little money, but not in New York.

My obsession with the internet became worse as real life beat us down. I slipped further into it. My online friends became more important than the physical people in my life. Message boards and chat rooms were like corner bars to pop into before going home for the night, and, like the corner bar, I spent all my time there.

Online poker gave me the same high as any other drug. The web answers every need. If you're hungry, angry, lonely or tired, the internet has thousands of sites that will help, and more to recover.

"I drop everything and walk away once in a while." Jeff Wimbelton said.

"I was thinking of doing just that."

"It did wonders for me."

#

My next big break from the internet lasted one day. I busied myself with food, and only checked e-mails, but, Matt called. "Hey man, you need to check your book page. Bennison posted an apology on it."

"Really?"

"Yeah, he was banned from the Elan School page, and he's started his own group."

44

"Him?"

"That's what I was thinking."

The monster was at the door again, waving an olive branch and talking about forgiveness. I friended him, but wasn't fooled. He was up to something, and I found it right away. I checked his friend list and Facebook wall and found a writer. I checked her out, and knew I was being played.

I told Matt and he posted about Danny writing a book on the Elan group on Facebook, so when the time came I would have proof that I knew. Danny said he wanted to advocate against abusive programs together, so I joined his group and played along.

\#

I asked Matt, "What happened to Jimmy Shiplett?"

According to him, ex Elan staff director Ken Zaretsky handed a gun to a very drunk Jimmy Shiplett and told him that the police had his girlfriend, Cathy, and if he wanted her back he needed to go in and demand her back at gunpoint. Jimmy tried, but was killed by a shotgun blast to the chest.

"Zaretsky was pulled back into Elan for it, and he told me what happened." Matt said. "They took Jimmy's motorcycle and dumped it on the side of the interstate, and got Zaretsky as far away from the investigation as possible."

"And, Elan was as far as you needed to be."

"I'm afraid so."

"But why?" I was confused. "What was so special about them?"

Even the Catholic Church couldn't escape the scrutiny of child abuse, yet Elan was closed for months and no one would speak negatively about them. There were no lawyers or lawsuits to fear anymore but people in the media still didn't say the truth.

"You can start by asking Senator Bill Diamond." Matt said. "He was in Elan up to his neck."

"I'll check him out."

"Getting back to Jimmy Shiplett...This is the strangest part. Mark sent me the article about his death, and the article is dated nineteen seventy five, but I know for a fact he was killed in nineteen seventy four." Matt went on to wonder if the article was submitted a year late, or it had been changed during the introduction to the internet. "Whatever happened, I can tell you for sure it was seventy four."

There was one other death I had heard about when I was a resident. A kid died in the Elan Seven dorm from breathing in dust, and the story had no rumor attached to it, so it figured that was what happened. Still, they were careful to keep people quiet about it because dead kids close down residential treatment programs.

I asked Matt his opinion of why Straight survivors protested and sued the owners and none of us had. He told me that a former resident sued Joe Ricci and won, but she was under a non-disclosure agreement, so the details weren't revealed. "By then, she had enough and just took the money."

"And it continued."

"Yeah."

#

The first difference I saw about Straight Inc. is that the family was involved with the program and treatment. That was so far from what we experienced that it jumped out at me. Straight used the family to make more money by pulling in siblings, and threatening the parents. The people who worked there were very skilled at emotional abuse and blackmail. Parents didn't escape the long arm of therapy.

In Elan, it was rare to have contact with family for at least a year. In many cases it was longer. Phone calls were short, and staff listened to the conversation. "That's illegal." Matt said. ""But so is wrapping a young girl up like a mummy and throwing her in the lake."

"They really did that?"

"They did it to Jennifer Stamler. She was Gerald Davidson's niece."

"Really?"

"Yup, and that sick piece of shit ran the general meeting himself."

"You don't hear a lot about Davidson."

"Well, Davidson was rarely there, and he left in the mid-eighties."

"Strange, that."

Doctor Gerald Davidson opened Elan with Joe Ricci, and from eyewitness accounts he was as bad as Joe, but by the late 70s he only did intakes, and in 1986 he walked away from Elan altogether.

"There were over 300 residents in eighty six." I said.

"He walked away with millions."

"He also walked away from millions. Easily three or four million a year for twenty five years. A hundred million dollars maybe."

"Wow."

"That violates every tenant of a greedy sadistic child abuser."

"Maybe he developed a conscience."

"He wrapped his niece up like a mummy and had residents throw her in the lake. People like that don't develop a conscience."

"True."

"Besides, if he developed a conscience he would have spoken up. Maybe published something."

"You got that right."

\#

Liz said it many times and I listened when she did and nodded and agreed. "Write the Elan book."

As I learned more about the industry it became an obsession. From Synanon to the present day wilderness programs, it was a great story. The problem was that it was another abuse story, and people hate abuse stories.

I had two romance novel ideas, and started one, only to lose interest at fifty thousand words. I started two nonfiction proposals and lost interest in them as well, so I changed directions and read all I could find about behavior modification, and processed it for the book that I couldn't ignore.

"The Game." I said.

Liz looked confused.

"The name of my next book."

She shrugged. "Then, write it."

And I tried.

\#

Writers say that when you get tangled up, to keep writing and come back to it, but until the first paragraph is perfect I can't. Coming back to fix it is not an option. I wished it wasn't so, but it was and I couldn't change it. After I'm satisfied with the first paragraph, I tend to write quickly for a person who types with two fingers. Up to ten thousand words a day.

There was so much to tell and so many ways to tell it, but with The Game, my usual routine failed me. It was backwards. I nailed the first paragraph and went into complete writer's block.

Writers argue the writer's block theory well, so I believe and don't believe it exists according to how I feel that day. But, I had never experienced it until then. When it hit, I couldn't write a word.

"Nothing?" Liz said.

"Nothing."

Every day I sat in front of the computer and stared at the computer screen with a cup of tea and three cigarettes. Nothing came to me but bad thoughts. I didn't feel safe. My head spun from the worry of what Danny or my brother had up their sleeves.

"Why don't you try doing writing prompts?"

I razzed that.

"How about flash fiction, or fanfic?"

"I've done fan fuck."

"Huh?"

"It's erotica with celebrities."

She laughed. "Stop, I'm serious."

"So am I. I've got a dozen of them."

"Really? Who?"

I told her, and she laughed, so I explained, but Liz hated to talk about sex, so I gave her the less graphic details. "I think they'd sell, but I would get sued."

"Back to this one then...."

Liz was as stressed by our living situation as me. She understood it was her fault, but didn't have an answer to our problem. The reason was simple: there wasn't one. We were stuck.

She sighed. "I wish I could tell you to write, but under this stress I don't think anyone could."

I always enjoyed the sound a can of beer made when someone cracked the seal. Ka-poosh. It made everyone happy. In our room in Queens, New York, I learned to hate it. He drank two beers at a time, so it was always a matter of time before he went into an angry rant, and we had to sit and pray that he wouldn't knock on our door to vent it on us, and more times than not he did.

"I'm afraid of that man." She sat on the end of the bed. "I'm a woman. I shouldn't have to live like this."

All the bills were months behind, and the rent was one month in arrears, and we had paid our share of it, so when it came to putting up or shutting up he attacked, and blamed us. My father bailed him out in the end, but it repeated the following month. It was hell.

"I think I can write this book, even in the middle of this chaos."

"Do ya?"

"Sure." I sat at my desk. "If you remember, this whole thing started out as a suicide note."

VI

A member of my writer's group told me it was likely that Danny Bennison had no idea who I was, and Danny sounded sincere when he said he lay awake at night trying to remember me, so I was baffled. How can you rape and torture someone and not remember their name? I was very important to him for a few months, 30 years before, but my writer friend said I was an object to him, and his recall rejected or changed memories of his crimes. She called it, "Confabulation."

There was no doubt that joining Danny's group would raise eyebrows, but I had already gotten him to admit to rape and needed to see if I could get him to admit something else.

"He drinks or does drugs from the look of some of his posts. He'll slip up and say something stupid."

Liz was concerned. "You should go talk to someone."

"About him?"

"About you."

Psychiatrists and therapists were a waste of time and money. I knew what they were going to say, and knew when they were lying to me. New York City Medicaid only covered clinical care, which was competent to handle typical psyche patients, which I wasn't.

"I could do their job, and better."

"Probably."

I changed the subject. "Did you know they could have put me through Harvard for the same amount of money they spent to send me to Elan?"

Jeff Wimbelton showed me a chart of the things the state of Connecticut could have done with the money. Schooling, vacations, stocks, bonds, and retirement accounts. "The government was willing to pay, fifty, sixty, seventy thousand dollars on a therapy they knew was flawed—"

"Abusive." I interrupted.

""Abusive." He agreed. "And look at the good they could have done."

"But, why?"

"I don't know. It doesn't make sense."

The people who knew and continued to subject kids to behavior modification also knew it might tarnish their reputations forever. Doctor Gerald Davidson had his legacy to consider, which may have factored into his departure from Elan. My searches on the internet brought up nothing about him. I didn't understand.

"Someone needs to find this guy's story."

"That someone is you." Jeff said. "You're getting good at this."

I didn't know how to write it, but Jeff told me it would come to me, which I didn't usually doubt. I couldn't put anything on paper. Whether or not writer's block existed, it existed in my head, which made it real. It was the literary equivalent of trying not to think of the color blue. At the same time, my OCD wanted me to write—it was maddening.

#

"I'm going to take a vacation from writing." I turned off the computer by pressing the button they warn you not to press. "Why do I need to write every day?"

"You can read." Liz said.

"I will when I get back from my appointment. I have to see Krista in twenty minutes."

Krista was my forensic psychologist at Catholic Charity's psych clinic in Woodside, Queens. She had red hair and milk-white skin, and a pretty face. She was soft spoken and sweet, but there was something wrong between us. She was smart, so the relationship felt like it had potential, but there was something not right, and I couldn't figure out what it was.

The best way to lose a psychiatric professional is to tell them that you had been kidnapped by the government, taken to an isolated location and beaten, tortured and brainwashed. What none of them considered was that I was the one in a million who was telling the truth. I figured that was what was getting in our way.

I told her about my books, and writer's block. "I can't read, write, nothing. It's like my brain has shut down. Not one more bit of information in, and not one bit out. I'm numb." I said.

She asked me about things that trigger my anxiety, and solutions to those, and ended our session by asking if I had any ideas of suicide, to which I answered, "no," and then if I had any ideas of hurting someone else. She sat up when she asked.

"No."

"Okay, then. Just want to be sure…After the last session…"

Krista took my information in our earlier meeting. She asked the usual questions, and I was determined to tell the truth because my symptoms were bad for the first time in years, so when she asked me about suicidal thoughts, I told her that after forty years of wanting to kill myself I had it under control, and that if I should hit crisis mode I would call her or 911.

She was satisfied, and asked if I ever had ideas of hurting or killing others, and I said, "Sure, doesn't everybody?" and that was the wrong answer considering I had told her earlier that I had been kidnapped by the government, taken to a remote location and beaten tortured and brainwashed.

Krista wore low cut blouses, so that was something else getting in the way of our relationship. I liked it and didn't, because my mind was in crisis, but she knew what she was doing because she covered up when she bent over, so she was teasing and though I liked that, I didn't. The rest of the staff was beautiful women, and I was doomed to fall for whoever they switched me to, so I didn't ask for a different doctor.

The sessions were mercifully short and once a week, so it wasn't too bad, but I was getting nothing out of going. It was a checkpoint for them, to possibly catch me before I blew. Krista was the same as the rest in one respect: she had no idea what to do with me.

#

53

Liz was angry, understandably, that I wanted to join Danny Bennison's Facebook group for Elan survivors. We discussed his abuses many times, but I kept one truth from her. No one but Danny and I knew what happened in his office the day he raped me. It was my only secret from her.

"I'm aware he's probably up to something, but you never know. "

When I found Danny posing in the survivor group, by all indications he was getting along with people. I wondered if my appearance on the scene might have ruined an honest effort to make up for his past. Matt laughed and told me Danny was vicious and threatened people on the internet, and mentioned again that Danny had threatened him.

"It's in that Diablo article." He said. "And, if you look at his profile on Fornits, he's deleted half of his posts. He does that when he sobers up in the morning."

"Internet post guilt."

"Sort of, but with Bennison it's more like he's hiding his tracks."

"Well, I'm going to stick around and see what's what for myself."

"What's what is he's a snake. Believe me."

#

When lawsuits and litigation closed down Straight Inc. they changed names and opened up in other locations. When Elan closed I asked around and found the ways Straight survivors kept tabs on them and found their new programs. A survivor named Sue told me that there is a Straight based program in Alberta called AARC, and that they tracked company names and real estate holdings. I wondered if Elan was planning on reopening in another location.

That night, Jeff sent me a message. ""Have Mark Babitz check out Golden Ark, and states with weak regulations for troubled teens, like Texas or Utah."

We got a hit for Texas right away, and in the days that followed we found two more. "Golden Ark is Elan, there's no doubt." Matt said.

"That's for sure." Mark said.

I wasn't skeptical, but was unconvinced we could do anything. "What can we do if it's true?"

"We hammer them until they close their doors." Mark said.

Matt agreed.

According to them Sharon Terry owned Golden Ark, but there was no indication she planned to use the property for anything but rentals. Of course she could rent it to herself and use her contacts in the industry to open a wilderness program, or another therapeutic community.

"She would have to get licenses for that."

"She could hire a psychiatrist to run it for her." Matt said. "Hide it that way."

There was no way to be completely sure. There were hundreds of programs around the country who used varied methods of Elan's brutal insanity. Eventually, programs began popping up in other countries. Kids from the United States were flown to abuse mills in foreign countries, where they had no more rights than a convicted criminal.

Casa by the Sea was closed down in 2004 by Mexican police and child protection services, and then U.S. Congressman George Miller asked the State Department to take action against World Wide Association of Specialty Programs and Schools, or WWASPS, for abuse of American children on foreign soil.

Tranquility bay was another WWASPS program closed by lawsuits and abuse complaints. They blamed declining enrollment, as Elan had claimed. Tranquility Bay is considered one of WWASPS toughest abuse mills. In 2001, a young inmate committed suicide, and staff treated it as an accident, though the young lady left a suicide note.

The advocates who fought abusive programs called it, "The Troubled Teen Industry," and the stories were as bizarre as the ones I remembered from Elan, and so the guilt of never having spoken up kicked in again. I wrote to Danny and told him that I was willing to bury the hatchet if he would work with me to fight abusive programs, and he agreed.

\#

Kelly Matthews tipped me off to Mitt Romney's connection to WWASPS through political connections, and his involvement with Aspen Group, another corporate version of Elan. The stories of abuse were all over the internet. Mitt Romney owned Bain Capital, and Bain owned Aspen.

Romney was getting ready to kick off his campaign in Florida, and Florida made me think of Straight Inc. and the owner Mel Sembler's political connections. I found a Miami newspaper article that had Mel at Mitt's side, and named as his chief money man.

"We have to spread the word." Kelly said.

"I'm on it."

We started by posting on all the troubled teen sites and Facebook pages, and then called Romney out on his own page for having a child abuser as a fund raiser. We were eventually banned. Undiscouraged, I went to the Barak Obama Facebook page and let them know the good news: that we had found dirt on his opponent. I was banned from that page as well.

"They've all got their hands in the pie. Both parties." Matt said.

"Then how do you fight it?"

"Just keep doing what you're doing."

\#

"I Survived the Horrors of Aspen Ranch," sounds like a place for people who were horrified by Aspen Ranch, but upon arrival I saw that newcomers who voiced negative opinions about the place were attacked with vile language and accusations.

My experience caused me to post the following article on Reddit:

When I was invited to join the Face Book group, "I survived the horrors of Aspen Ranch" it seemed simple. I had done it with similar program survivor groups, and had introduced myself as an Elan survivor who was a supporter of their cause, but it was clear right away that this

Aspen Ranch group is different. I had heard about victims being attacked by pro program people, and ex staff members, and experienced it myself, but I had never seen a group run by them. It got bad right away.

The first post on the group was one by someone who said she had never done drugs before Aspen Ranch, and the first three people to comment had the same experience. The fourth comment disturbed me. Sallie Gill said this, "prolly cause you thought u were a bad ass when u were just a winey bitch who drove our whole team crazy. Too bad you threw a great opportunity away. But hey it's your life to waste and you only get one." And then she said, "Glad all the fuck ups stay on the one side. Makes it easier to do well in life."

I followed by asking her if she was an abuser. Her language and attitude warranted the question. Any survivor or reasonable person would agree. Sallie blocked me rather than answer, so her silence was answer enough. It didn't end there. That was my introduction to Amber Speiss, (abuser) an ex staff member.

A quick search came up with this from Heal Online (a.k.a. Aspen Education Group-- Confirmedly Abusive and Associated with the CEDU Cult Model) Amber Spiess (Bailey) Residential Supervisor has been with Aspen since 2000.

The horrors of Aspen Ranch are still going on. The group is nothing more than an attempt to lure in and silence survivors. The administrators support it and attack anyone who defends the victim. Amber Speiss attacked me for saying that I was helping a former victim of Aspen to write a book. She didn't ask what the book is about, and didn't care, because she knows it is about abuse. How could it not be? Though there are people who say Aspen saved their life, there are survivor stories online, so even if it did, it doesn't negate the experiences of those who were destroyed by it. Experts on brainwashing will tell you that people claim that prison saved their life.

Back to Amber Speiss. She started off with the usual program defense, that I was after a quick buck and had an agenda. I told her that I won't get a penny, and that I was only commenting on Sallie's abusive post, calling people, "Whiney bitches" and "Fuck ups" but Amber called me a liar. I linked her to my book, A Life Gone Awry, and showed her that I won't even get money for that. The proceeds will go to CAFETY and Program Watch, to fight for the rights of children in abusive programs. Amber's response was typical.

"But you're not affiliated with ANYONE, specifically CAFETY. Gottcha. Your story changes by the minute and I'm ending my part of this conversation. Too inconsistent. Stay objective, Wayne, let ALL the kids have their say, that you perp on."

Amber thinks she's a good manipulator and liar, which is true, but only when applied to children. My agenda was to help abuse victims, and that enrages her. What does that say about her, and Aspen Ranch? Aspen was closed because of abuse. The pro Aspen bunch says it was because of decreased enrollment, but they forget to mention why enrollment decreased. The reason is because parents now have the internet, and they check out the places they are told to send their children. Aspen Ranch is closed because of abuse, end of story.

I left the group, only to be attacked and called a piece of shit, by a foul mouthed little girl from New Milford, Connecticut, named, Noelle. A psychology student at Baldwin-Wallace College. Noelle blocked me so that I couldn't see her remark, a typical internet troll tactic. When a friend defended me, she blocked him and deleted her comment. This is the action of a person who did well at Aspen. Another testament to its abuse and brainwashing.

Then there's Steve Burr (abuser). This was posted by one of Steve's victims. "Steve-you're a worthless piece of shit...I remember one time when blaze(small ass twelve year old) was so sick we had to help him walk to the dining hall .when he got there he couldn't lift his head off the table to talk to you ,the greatest person on earth in bum fuck Utah, that you and that dumb ass hoe Robin (terrible cook) twisted his arms behind his back so hard he was crying in front of the main house for like an hour straight. You could hear the screams from the barn even. So fuck you you're a fat ass and haven't accomplished shit with your life except for tormenting children at a horrible place that lies completely to the parents and charges ridiculous prices...so fuck off."

But what is the word of one survivor? It was enough to attract this response from another victim. "If yall only knew how bad it was when I was there. What you said happened to blaze was a daily thing."

Steve Burr hurt and abused children, and he joined the group to try to shut me up with his ridiculous program hogwash, but Steve (abuser) didn't know he was dealing with an adult who would bury him if he tried to twist my arm behind my back. He changed his tune when I told him I know he is living in Axtell, Utah, and I know where his wife works. The internet is a wonderful source of information.

The Face Book group, "I survived the horrors of Aspen Ranch" is abusive and hateful. A quick scroll down the group wall shows people being called, "Faggot," "Bitch," "Asshole," Crack whore," "Cunt," and more. Of course, you can't scroll down their group wall because as soon as I told Steve (abuser) that I was writing this article, they closed the group so that you can't see the truth, and the truth is that they behave hatefully, and are horrible to anyone they don't like. I can't close down their group, but since it is listed on Fornits Wiki as a survivor group, I won't stop trying to expose it, and I'm asking for your help.

Picture a Straight Inc, Kids of Bergen County, WWASP, or similar group, set up to do this exact same thing to you, and picture Miller Newton, Mel Sembler or Robert Lichfield calling you a whiney bitch, a Faggot or a baby, and ask what you would want someone to do for you. If you've never been to a program, you've certainly come across an internet bully or two. Ask yourself the same thing.

Please, for one day, spread the word about "I survived the horrors of Aspen Ranch," and help a survivor who may fall into the hands of these predators. It's the right thing to do.

#

Most of the comments have been deleted, but a fight broke out on the Reddit page, and false allegations were made against me. A private message was posted on the Aspen group page that exposed me as an advocate for the troubled teen industry, and I asked the question that stopped all Aspen defenders from posting.

"I wonder if the judge presiding in the civil trial might see this group as possible witness tampering."

The group deleted me and my friends, and the story sunk into the murk of the internet. People didn't know what to do. I didn't know what to do either. The one good thing that came of it was the private message that was posted. It stated, "Wayne is full of balony…" and that was Danny Bennison's bad spelling, so I knew he was full of shit. I also knew it made me useless as an advocate

"I don't have the temperament for this." I told Matt.

"Wayne, you're a writer. Go write. These Aspen creeps are just like the Elan creeps." He paused, and then said, "You know it was Danny who wrote that private message, right?"

"Yup."

I wanted to quit Danny's group and walk away, but there was a discussion going on that interested me more. A former Synanon leader had decided to tell his story. It was a firsthand account of the beginning of the madness.

"This guy thinks Synanon was the greatest thing that ever happened." Mark said.

There was a storm brewing in Danny's group.

VII

No one knew what to think when Ben Parks posted about Synanon on our Facebook group. Mark wanted to attack him because his initial comment was demeaning. Ben said that if we had been subjected to Synanon's game, we would have ended up in a rubber room playing handball with our own shit.

"This guy doesn't know Elan." Mark said in a private message. "He thinks we were in a kiddie Synanon."

"Let's see where this goes." I wrote. "It's interesting, if nothing else."

"Well, I'm going to go after him when he's done telling his story. He's pro-Synanon."

"Have at it, but let's hear him out first."

"Okay."

Ben's story was similar to what I had read on Paul Morantz's blog until the end. When his story wound down he said that people from the academic elite and the Human Potential Movement were interested in Synanon, and that the government was giving Chuck Dederich money under the table.

I wrote to Matt. "What's the human potential movement?"

"I don't know. Maybe you ought to get Mark to check them out."

"I'll do that."

"And, for your own good, when this is over you should quit that group and block Bennison." He went on about what a sick, twisted criminal Danny is, but I couldn't read it. I was disappointed. Danny looked like he was really getting into fighting for program survivors. He seemed to care, and was good at it. But, in the end he was a snake, and the people who told me not to get involved with him were right.

"I know." I said. "He's no good, but let me see if I can get any information out of him before I expose him. He sent me this back in March."

\#

Date: March 28

Subject: Yvette Portella

Just some inside information, Yvette and I had a thing while we were residents, while I was in re-entry and while I was staff. Which is one of the reasons why I left E-7 so abruptly. Yes we did hook up after she left. Her brother almost killed me along with her cousins they did not like white guys in New Haven.

This is the truth. I loved her a great deal. I got my heart broken big time.

Hey I don't want to fight with you. I am asking for forgiveness for crimes I can't remember, honestly Wayne. I have had sleepless nights trying to remember you, I don't. I have a family and a business so I am very careful about things that would harm them. I know you can understand this.

Let's just lay the swords down and let this go for a while and work at shutting Elan down. Maybe in time we can see more of each other's souls through our writings here. Many of the people that support your book are my friends some are not. But they asked me how I felt about them supporting your book, I said go for it this is between Wayne and I. Ya see Wayne no one else has wrote a book we could show people so they could read what went on in Elan. Not as explicit as yours. You know you're not done writing there is so much more to tell. You are a great writer and Elanians need someone like you to tell their story, please collaborate with others get the real info and get it out there. I believe until Sharon, Jeff and Marty see their names written out there they won't shut down Elan.

Thanks for reading if you did,

Take care

Danny

#

The rumor in 1978 was that Joe Ricci and Jeff Gottlieb had locked a gay kid and a young girl in a room with two convicted rapists and told them to do whatever they wanted, and they raped them repeatedly, which prompted Danny to threaten Yvette Portella in a general meeting.

Yvette was fifteen or sixteen years old, which made her a minor, and Danny was her director, which made having sex with her statutory rape, but his threat in that general meeting made it rape. If his claim was true, she had sex with him under duress—she had no choice.

"If I walk out of here, and let you people do what you want, who would rape this bitch?" He said.

For a few seconds no one raised their hand, but it was obvious Danny wasn't going to stop until someone did. It was only going to get worse if we didn't play along. I was the first to raise my hand. Yvette looked at me when I did, and the hurt in her eyes was unbearable.

Other hands went up until the majority of the men were part of Danny's sick fear tactic. I didn't know until he sent that message that he used that fear to force her into having sex with him. There was little doubt that if she didn't, he would have subjected her to the same treatment that Joe Ricci and Jeff Gottlieb had done to the two children they locked up and had raped.

"That was the only guilt I took with me when I left Elan."

"It wasn't your fault." Matt said. "You were a kid. You were afraid."

"I was a fucking coward."

"What were you supposed to do, stand up to that psycho piece of shit?"

In the two years I spent at Elan, most of the time I had been in trouble or in low positions of authority. It was torturous and frustrating while it went on, but it left me with a mostly clean conscience after I left. The only thing worse than being beaten and tortured was that Elan made us beat and torture each other. It caused many to keep quiet about what happened there, and many assuaged their guilt by rationalizing what happened there as necessary punishment.

"I'm going to get that son of a bitch for this…He thinks A Life Gone Awry was bad. Wait till I tell the world he's a sexual predator."

"He belongs in jail, with Jeff Gottlieb and Marty Kruglick and Sharon Terry." Matt said. "There are a lot of people who aren't dancing on this planet because of those criminals."

I knew in my heart that it wasn't my fault, but the guilt wouldn't go away. That night, for the first time in seven years, I got drunk and cut myself.

#

When Ben's Synanon story was done a fight broke out. He was called out for being a Synanon apologist, and admiring Chuck Dederich, but I remembered what I read on Paul Morantz's blog. Ben said that Synanon was once a beautiful and productive community, which strived to be held in high esteem by its neighbors and felt as if it was as near to a paradise as he'd ever seen. But, then it began to go totally insane.

I stayed out of the fight until the end, then posted that I believed Ben wasn't pro-Synanon, and that he didn't understand what happened to the Game after the government shut Synanon down. "I don't think you realize what we went through, Ben."

I wrote. "I feel like I'm being talked to by staff. Not like you're abusive, but because you don't get it…We went to Elan. The people who played handball with their own shit were afraid of us."

The fight ended, and we told Ben about Elan's abuse. Mark told about the boxing ring, and how it was more of a beat down than a punishment. Linda told about the spankings, and I chimed in about the paddle and the blood and bruises. We described how ten to twenty residents would kick and beat someone, which was called a cowboy ass kicking.

"I saw Marty make a crown of tampons and dip them in ketchup, and put them on a girl's head." Linda said. "It was sick."

"I watched them beat Michael Blackman for months, claiming he was faking mental illness to get out." I said.

"They did that to Jennifer Stamler." Matt said.

Ben became properly horrified by Elan and its sick adaptation of the Game, and agreed that Elan was insane—far worse than he thought—and we discussed what to do about it.

"Well, I'm an old man, and I'm disabled." I said. "But I'm not done kicking ass yet. I was reading a story in the New York Times about an autistic kid who was killed in the Oswald Heck center, and the piece of shit who killed him sat on him and said, "I can be a good king or a bad king," and they beat this kid all day with a stick, and called it, "the magic stick"….Tell me that isn't Elan language."

The group agreed it was.

"Faced with all that, the staff still wouldn't admit this shit was abuse."

"That's fucked up." Mark said.

"Elan treated autistic kids. I'm convinced someone came along and saw what they were doing and started using it on them."

"I read that story." Linda said. "They were getting over a million dollars a year to take care of that boy."

"His name was Jonathan Carey." I said. "Could you imagine what was going through his head? Could you imagine what was going through Jennifer Stamler's mind? Michael Blackman? Danny Broach? Any of the rest?"

"What do you want to do?" Ben said.

"I want to get these fuckers. Make their worst nightmare come true, and expose them. Who's with me?"

"I am."

"Me too."

"I'm in."

And so it began.

\#

Liz took me out to coffee that night after my brother had left for work and showed me the envelope the landlord left in the mailbox on the first of every month. It showed that he was two months in arrears. Then, she showed me copies of the bills, which were the same.

"What do you want me to do? He's fucking psycho."

"He's not that crazy. He knows right from wrong."

I agreed. "He knows it's wrong when someone does it to him."

Liz was convinced that Kenny used the fear he created in people by acting crazier than he actually was to get his way. I suspected that because he had never been put in a hospital or went crazy and got arrested. At our sister's wedding he beat up our brother Charlie, who he outweighed by fifty pounds, but put his hands behind his back when the cops arrived.

"He's a bully and a coward."

"Well, he's bullying me." Liz said. "So, I'm going to get an order of protection against him from the domestic violence detectives at the precinct."

"My family will flip, but fuck it. They make excuses for him. I'll back you up a hundred percent."

\#

It seemed easy before I began advocating for abused children. Post evidence of torture, rape and death. Post pictures of kids in dog cages, and lists of dead children. It should have horrified people into supporting the closure of abusive programs, and created a call for regulation in residential treatment programs. But nothing is as easy as it seems. I hadn't considered the fact that most people didn't understand, and some didn't care.

When the New York Times ran an online article about the torture and abuse of terror suspects, the commenters had two sides. Both brought up compelling issues. When Matt and I entered the discussion, we were called trolls and told to go away. This was by a person who was against the torture, even for the coercion of life-saving information.

I posted the link to the trailer for Surviving Straight Inc. and asked, "Why should it be illegal to do this to people who are a threat to our country, but not for children in therapeutic treatment?"

"Why should we believe a bunch of lying drug addicts?"

I posted links to evidence. "The same treatment you're arguing against is being used on kids. Beatings, torture and brainwashing."

"Brainwashing? Now you just sound like an idiot."

"Really?" I posted an excerpt from a 1974 press release that had been on the front page of many major newspapers.

#

"Other forms of behavior modification techniques employ intensive "encounter sessions" in which individuals are required to participate in group therapy discussions where intensive pressure is often placed on the individuals to accept the attitudes of the group... Once the individual is submissive, his personality can begin to be reformed around attitudes determined by the program director to be acceptable. Similar to the highly refined "brainwashing" techniques employed by the North Koreans in the early nineteen fifties, the method is used in the treatment of drug abusers... "The Seed", a drug abuse treatment program in Florida that, until recently, received funding from the Department of Health, Education, and Welfare, is based on a similar philosophy."

INDIVIDUAL RIGHTS AND THE FEDERAL ROLE IN BEHAVIOR MODIFICATION by the COMMITTEE ON THE JUDICIARY, UNITED STATES SENATE, Subcommittee on Constitutional Rights, November, 1974, pp. 15 - 16 describing The Seed.

#

"Children in this country are being beaten, raped and tortured. They deserve at least the same rights as someone who has planted a bomb in a major city with the intention of killing innocent citizens." I said.

Rather than respond, the man left the discussion. A few of the people there showed interest, so we showed them the videos, and blogs, and linked them to articles about the horror that is being called therapy.

"I was in the Elan School." Matt said. "And I can tell you people from firsthand experience that your children are being destroyed on a daily basis. Somewhere, someone is being subjected to Elan's sick form of abuse right now. We're not trolls; we're trying to do something about it."

When the discussion ended we had gotten the message to a few people, but it took hours and didn't do much for my morale. I knew it would be an uphill battle, but had no idea how tough it was going to be. Matt reassured me, but depression had me by the throat.

"The most frustrating thing is that these people immediately assume the kids are liars."

"Yeah, they said the same thing about Elan survivors." Matt said.

"And people still believe it."

"They can't call us liars anymore. They convicted a man of murder and threw him in prison based on Elan Survivor's testimony."

They did do that.

VIII

In February of 1974 Chuck Dederich admitted that using Synanon's game on children was experimental. He also justified physical attack therapy because he was roughed up as a kid in a Jesuit high school. He called it, "House breaking," and said that smart ass kids needed to be knocked on their asses once in a while.

When Synanon became a church, the question left unanswered was, "Who will be God?" but not because people were afraid to ask—it was because the question didn't need to be asked. It was assumed. Charles E. Dederich was the Lord Almighty.

Dederich liked the idea of becoming a church right off, and had Howard Garfield and Steve Simon develop it. He called them, "The Harvard Boys."

"Harvard, eh?"

"Yeah, Harvard. Why?" Liz handed me the laptop.

"Nothing. I just keep seeing Harvard."

"Didn't the guy who owned Elan go to Harvard?"

"He was a professor."

"Look him up."

Doctor Gerald Davidson was nowhere to be found on the internet. It was another of Elan's great mysteries. "How could someone in business with Joe Ricci, with all his public exposure, lawsuits and gubernatorial campaign, not be all over the internet? Even Elan people didn't talk about him."

"Forget that." Liz said. "Why isn't he published?"

"What do you mean?"

"There's one rule at Harvard. Publish or perish."

According to her, to remain as Harvard faculty you have to publish articles and books, so I took the question to the best researchers I knew—the posters on Fornits. In no time I had three articles co-written by Davidson.

Liz laughed. "He has to do way better than that to be a psychology professor."

I checked his cowriters and found they were all published. There were links to Amazon and Barnes & Noble, and newspaper and magazine articles. I did another search of his name with more specific search terms, and didn't even hit on the discussion we were having on Fornits.

"I'm going to ask my brother about this." Liz picked up her laptop. "I want to know how he was teaching at Harvard with only those three articles to his name."

"Cool, thank you."

#

When I took the sexual abuse out of A Life Gone Awry, I knew that one day I would probably tell the story, and that people would question my veracity. I knew when I put it on Fornits that someone I respected might call the question. That person was Paul St. John.

I explained:

"I haven't been posting here, but I have been reading. I'll make the exception because it's you asking the question Paul

First, I knew people weren't going to believe me when I said this. That made it harder to say. I've been instructed not to engage Danny, so when he posts here I can't reply to any questions, so I'll be clear. Every word of what I said is true. I didn't put it in the book because I was ashamed. I also knew how he was going to react. When he realized who I was on the phone he became evil. All those posts about my ass and stripping me naked, and shooting my load were to bully me into not saying it. I knew he was going to attack my sexuality and blame the victim. As he did with the sexual fantasy post he started

Read the first post in the thread I started. It will take you 15 minutes. He admitted to it with Yvette.

*I don't misunderstand your doubt, but keep your mind open. If someone accused me of
this I'd have called the police. He's afraid of an investigation. He's guilty."*

#

"You knew this was going to happen." Liz kissed my forehead. "I'm sorry you have to go
through this."

Everything changed after that. The anxiety and urgency in my mind calmed and I was
able to sleep and eat properly. My time on the internet became more normally balanced with real
life. People believed my story, and others didn't—that will never change.

Danny behaved so badly that he convinced many that I was telling the truth. First, he
made fun of the accusation, then, started a thread in which he claimed I had sexual fantasies
about him. When I reminded him that I was fifteen years old, he abandoned that and made fun of
my sexuality—a typical tactic for a sexual predator.

Finally, I said, "Dan, it's this simple." I posted the number and address for the 108th
Precinct. "Call the precinct, and tell them that I've accused you of raping children, and they'll
come over here, and if I can't show them proof, they'll arrest me and throw me in jail. What are
you waiting for?"

Instead of answering, he created fake profiles and called me a faggot and accused me of
never having been in Elan. Though everyone on that site knew it was him and told him so, he
continued. It became clear that he was drinking or getting high, so eventually I gave up. He had
turned into an internet punching bag, and I began to look like an abuser again.

#

I was done with it. The darkest part of the darkest chapter of my life was over. I faced it
and didn't falter. I told the story and was done with it. And, there is a place on the web that tells
the truth, which will be there until the internet falls. And the truth is that Danny Bennison raped
children when he was an assistant director at Elan.

"I believe you." Matt said.

71

"Yeah, but what bothers me is that son of a bitch tried to push a girl to kill herself so he could blame me."

"She's not going to kill herself."

"I know, but he didn't, and he tried."

"Bennison is criminally insane."

"Well, fuck him." I said. "I'm onto a real criminal."

"Who's that?"

"The man who started this whole thing."

"Chuck Dederich?"

"Nope…Gerald Davidson."

IX

I copied and saved Ben Parks' Synanon discussion to my documents and highlighted the parts about the heavy hitters in the government and universities interested in the game. I reread it after Jeff and I discussed Gerald Davidson.

The Human Potential Movement was of special interest to me because I had a very high IQ. "Most people in Elan were smart as fuck. Even the ones who couldn't read or write were highly intelligent. Maybe they were experimenting on gifted kids."

Liz shrugged. "Maybe. Why don't you look up this human potential movement and check them out?"

I had their Wiki page up. "I am, and what I keep seeing is Harvard."

"Really?"

"Sure, check it out. " I stood. "Anthony Robbins was named one of the two hundred greatest businessmen ever by Harvard. William Shutz was Harvard faculty. Tim Leary, Harvard staff. Wavy Gravy, Harvard. It's amazing."

The member list put Human Potential Movement members at almost every major university in the state of California. Many others attended or taught on the east coast at one university in particular. "You really need to talk to your brother. These other people are all famous, but Davidson doesn't exist?"

"They weren't famous in the beginning." Liz said.

Behavior modification was controversial and Elan was too. It didn't make sense that a thorough Google search brought up almost nothing on Davidson. He should have been the famous one.

"What happened?"

"I have no idea." Liz said.

73

"When did he die?" I asked. "I can't even find anything about his death."

A poster with the screen name Ursus said, "Why don't you try putting M.D. after his name?"

"Was he an MD or a PHD?"

"Your doctor is an MD."

I found Doctor Davidson's obituary on the Journal of the American Medical Association website. It was the only thing aside from the co-written articles I had found with his name attached to it. The obituary said he went the Wayne State University, so I went to their alumni site and checked the list.

"Doctor Larry Brilliant." I said.

Liz looked up from her laptop. "What?"

"Doctor Larry Brilliant went to Wayne State around the same time as Gerald Davidson. Why do I know his name?"

"Isn't he that Google guy?"

I clicked on his Wikipedia page. "Yeah, that's the guy. He was also involved with the world health organization. They come up a lot too."

"Didn't they have a Nazi in charge once?"

"No, that was the world medical association."

In 1992, the American Medical Association was informed the president of the World Medical Association, Doctor Hans Sewering, was a member of Hitler's SS, and participated in Nazi euthanasia programs. He claimed there was a Jewish conspiracy against him, but was connected to a child who was sent to his death at Elfging-Haar. Nuns testified that euthanasia was carried out there, and as many as nine hundred children died there.

"I keep hearing that Hitler was a genius, but he was a fucking idiot."

"Why's that?"

"He fucked with the Jews."

"Never forget."

"You bet, and thank God for the Jews. What a piece of shit he was." I pointed to the computer screen. "Speaking of pieces of shit…"

Larry Brilliant was a co-founder of the Seva Foundation, as was Ram Dass, who was a Harvard psychology professor. Another Harvard connection was Wavy Gravy, who was good friends with Timothy Leary, who was also on the psychology department's faculty.

"What are the chances that Davidson was surrounded by human potential movement people, and had no idea?"

"Slim." Liz said.

People on Fornits rejected my idea that Davidson was running an experiment at Elan, and were convinced he was involved for the money, but if he was, why did he walk away when there were three hundred and fifty residents? His half of the money was close to five million dollars a year. Elan stayed in business for over twenty five years after he left.

"He said it didn't work." Matt said. "Maybe he lost interest."

"The only reason to walk away from a hundred million bucks was if his experiment was over and he wanted to get as far away as possible."

"You're probably right. He wanted to save his reputation."

"If he wanted to do that, he would have written something…Got himself published."

"He couldn't tell the world what happened in Elan."

"What if he lied?" I asked. "What if he couldn't print the truth about Elan?"

"Huh?"

"What if the truth is our greatest nightmare and the truth is that Elan's horrible therapy worked?"

\#

A visitor to my blog told me Pat Carlson was not the name of the kid who was in Elan 7 with me who murdered an eight year old boy and told the story in a general meeting. She told me his real name and the name of the victim. I searched them and got a hit right away.

On the Facebook group for the Burroughs School, a woman asked about the murder, and members reflected on the crime. One remembered that though Pat was the one who was caught; it was believed that he had an accomplice.

Mark sent me Pat's rap sheet, with a profile on the woman who asked the question. The rap sheet was mostly motor vehicle violations, drunk driving and switching license plates, or vehicle identification numbers.

"Didn't they get Ted Bundy for switching plates?" I asked.

"Nah, broken tail light."

"Still, this sounds like a guy who is trying to hide something."

"Or, he's a car thief."

Pat's rap sheet was interesting, but the woman who asked the question was more intriguing. According to what Mark was able to find, she worked for the sheriff's department where the crime occurred, which begged the question why she was trolling for information she could easily get herself.

I wrote her a private message, and said that I was in Elan with Pat, and would be happy to share what I knew about him, and the next morning she had blocked me from her Facebook profile. That was strange enough to get me to check the sheriff's department website, and when I did, I checked the cold case page, and there he was.

A young girl had been dragged into the woods and sodomized and next to the description of the crime was a composite drawing of the suspect, and it looked just like him. There was no doubt in my mind.

"That him." I told Mark. "The same rosy cheeks, the same big lips. We used to make fun of them, we called them,"Girly lips."

"Now we're getting somewhere."

"It's the same crime too, except he didn't kill this girl. Maybe he learned his lesson about murder."

"So, why did this chick from the sheriff's department block you? It doesn't make sense."

"Maybe she's afraid."

"Of who?"

"Well, the rumor back in Elan was that Pat was protecting his accomplice because he was the son of a cop."

"Now we're really getting somewhere."

#

I wrote to the sheriff's department about the cold case, and explained that the composite was the same person who was in Elan with me for a similar murder not long before the young girl was assaulted, and explained that he told the story of killing an eight year old boy with no emotion, and how his doctor said he would kill again and again.

The next morning the crime page on the sheriff's website was marked, "Solved," and the drawing of the suspect was gone. I called their office, and the man I spoke to told me the case had been solved for a long time, and he couldn't give me information over the phone. I asked about Pat's fugitive warrant.

"I can't comment on an open case."

I called mark, and he informed me that there was no more information available. "Serial killer or not, he was a juvenile when this happened."

"What if he didn't do it?"

"What do you mean?"

"What if the reason he told the story with so little emotion is because he wasn't the one who did it. Maybe he was describing what his partner did."

"That would make sense. What can we do about it?"

"Nothing, because I'm done with this. I'm not fucking with the cops."

"That's probably a good idea."

We discussed an alternative theory, which was that Pat was a sociopath and serial sexual predator and serial killer, but Elan had somehow cured him. "Maybe, they injected a conscience into him, and maybe inadvertently, Gerald Davidson had injected one into himself."

"That's crazy talk."

Pat wasn't the only murderer locked up with me at Elan. I had checked them all against prisoner lists all over the country and came up empty. As farfetched as the theory was, the odds against all of the child murderers in Elan never killing again was astronomical.

"It would explain why Elan stayed in business for forty one years."

#

When I hung up on Mark, it was time to deal with my brother. He had already taken rent from us for two months that he had not paid and was ready to take another, but Liz fought with him instead. When he stormed out of the apartment I went into his room to look for the rent envelope, but couldn't find it. What I found was my brother, Michael's diary.

In the summer of 1977, just before I was sent to Elan, Kenny, Michael and I camped out in the backyard, and the next day Michael told me that when I went into the house to get breakfast, Kenny had molested him. I told my parents and assumed that because of the delicacy of the matter it was dealt with quietly, but as I read the diary I found that it went on for years.

Kenny should have burned it, or shredded it, but he placed it on the bottom shelf of an alter he built around Michael's ashes. I put the diary back where I found it and took Liz out for coffee. She sat down and said, "Your brother is a sexual sadist."

"I know. What I want to know is why my parents did nothing about it."

"Guilt? Maybe one of them was the one who molested him."

"I don't think so."

"You've got a fucked up family, ya know that?"

"A lot of us did. Elan and Straight Inc. and places like it became a dumping ground for sexual abuse victims. Parents got rid of us as we got older to shut us up. Plus, programs labeled us as liars, so if we did say something, no one would believe us."

"That's horrible." Liz said.

"That's therapy."

X

The member list for the Human Potential Movement grew over time, putting them at almost every major university on the east and west coast. Stanford was popular in the west and Harvard in the east. Ben Parks mentioned Werner Erhard, so I looked him up, and learned about LGAT, or Large Group Awareness Training. Many say it is brainwashing, and it was what Elan was practicing, so I agreed.

The information on Werner Erhard showed that people either hated him or loved him. It was a Sunday morning when I found the book review editorial for, "How the Hippies Saved Physics," titled, "The Real Werner Erhard."

The author of the book had called Erhard, "The creepy Human Potential Movement guru," and the writer of the editorial attacked him for it, calling it inaccurate, and then told how brilliant he was, and a humanitarian. Then, he said that he went through EST, and served on staff of many of Erhard's enterprises.

"This guy is brainwashed." I said.

Liz shrugged. "Maybe he believes it was good, like those AA people who tell you their brain needed a little washing."

One thing in particular had been bothering me since I found out that Elan was practicing brainwashing techniques, so I told Liz that the people who ran Elan had predicted my life perfectly. They said I would end up addicted to drugs, end up in prison, and then end up on the streets prostituting myself for money.

"These people weren't qualified to sell shoes, but their insight was so great that they predicted my life? I don't believe it."

"You think they programmed your life into your head?"

"I don't know, but it's pretty interesting."

The author of the editorial finished by saying that Werner Erhard's bad reputation was shaped by lazy writers with hazy thinking, which made me more determined to show his hero for what he really was, which was far worse than creepy. First, I needed to find a direct link between him and Gerald Davidson.

I was OCD and an insomniac; I didn't have time for hazy thinking. And, I was anything but lazy.

#

Somehow, my brother knew that I had read Michael's diary. He didn't say it, instead, letting me know in the way he acted. Finally he blew up and the police were called. He lied and told them that we hadn't paid him the rent, and they believed him until Liz caught him in a lie. The reason he got mad when we paid all the bills without asking was because he was planning on abandoning the apartment. He told the cop that the electricity was being turned off because the bill wasn't paid, but Liz showed the cop the cancellation.

"Thank you for closing your account…" She said as she handed him the notice.

The cop she handed it to had just angrily and assuredly told me that I was wrong and the electricity was being turned off for non-payment, so he couldn't look at me. At that point the police were on our side, and as they left, one told Liz that if we needed him to testify to Kenny's lies, he would be happy to.

The next morning, Kenny packed a bag and left.

"Thank God." I said.

"Yeah."

#

"When did it become legal to do this to mentally ill kids?"

No one had an answer to that question. The kids CED was knocking to the ground to rattle their teeth were hardcore street kids addicted to heroin—they were a far cry from us. We had a few street toughs, but they were older residents and staff.

"Come to think of it, the only hardcore dope heads were staff when I left." Matt said.

Matt told me that it began to change while he was there, a few years before me. Danny wasn't the only one to see the change in residents from drug addicts to mentally ill and autistic kids. Matt saw it as well.

"When the state of Maine saw the opportunity to dump those kids on Elan they took it."

"Who gave the order? Someone had to sign some kind of release."

The rights of mentally ill kids were being closely scrutinized following the revelations of decades of experimentation on them. The stories were atrocious. "They gave LSD to mentally retarded kids. A hundred times the normal dose, every day, for months."

"That was the CIA and MKUltra." Matt said. "They ran a bunch of their experiments through Harvard."

"Harvard, eh?"

"Yeah. Doctor Gerald Davidson's alma mater, Harvard."

"Well, I'm rooting for Yale this year in the big game."

#

The Stanford Prison Experiment showed that you can take a normal person and put them in a position of power, and turn them into an abuser. Doctor Philip Zimbardo created a fake prison and the abuse became bad. A whistleblower halted the experiment as he sunk into it. The guards became abusive, and some of them loved it. I was interested because that was what happened in the woods of Maine at a place called, The Elan One Corporation.

Elan survivors agreed that the ones who were kept as staff were the ones who loved it. Danny Bennison had the personality. Marty Krugelik did too. They enjoyed what they were doing. Some deluded themselves into believing they were helping us, but most simply enjoyed hurting people.

"Maybe that's what they were doing to us. Trying to turn us into killers."

Mark laughed. "I doubt that's what they were doing, but that 'is' what ended up happening."

"Here's the thing that's bothering me. Davidson walked away from Elan when the money was at its peak. A guy who beats and tortures kids for money walked away from a hundred grand a week?"

"Like I told ya, he said Elan's therapy didn't work."

"Which sounds like the results of an experiment." He didn't say anything, so I continued. "What's the first thing you need to run an experiment like this?"

"I don't know."

"Control...Isolation."

"They certainly had that."

It begged the question of when Elan was given the go-ahead to beat and torture autistic kids. "Danny said it in his manifesto. They started bringing in mentally ill kids, autistic kids, and etcetera."

No one knew who gave that order.

"Find that person and you have your real criminal."

I asked Matt how Elan predicted my life perfectly. "I had never done drugs or ever been in trouble with the law, but two years after I graduated I was addicted and in prison. I had been in mental institutions, lived in the streets, and had prostituted myself for money."

"They brainwashed you." Matt said.

That made me think of Pat the child killer. "The entire time I was there with him, in Elan Seven, they told him that he was going to kill again."

"Wow." Matt said.

"Yeah."

I told him about the woman on the Facebook group and the sheriff's department, and that Mark and I thought it was a bad idea to mess with the police. Matt told me that I wasn't a crime fighter.

"You're a writer. Tell the story."

"That's my plan."

#

In the year we lived with Kenny, Liz and my relationship became bad. We fought all the time and I ranted when he was gone to work because I felt so stifled when he was home. My OCD became worse, and insomnia was a constant state.

Liz and I had always fought, and through it we survived crack and booze, poverty and abundance. We could say anything to each other and not hold it against each other. Love is forgiving someone for saying the unforgivable. What I said wasn't unforgivable, but it was the last thing either of us wanted to hear.

Liz asked if I wanted to break up, and I said, "From what? This has been over for a long time and you know it."

The truth drove away the anger and we were left with it. "It's not that I don't love you…I do. More than you'll ever know. "I kissed her forehead. "We got the best parts right. We love each other and we're good friends, but over the years it changed."

She frowned. "I love you too."

"I know."

"Ya know why?"

I shook my head.

"Because you have a great mind." She touched my head. "And, you have a great heart." She rested her hands on my shoulders. "And, you're a brilliant writer."

"I don't know how I put up with you."

She laughed. "Yeah, well, ditto."

#

People hated Danny and wanted to get away from him, and because he stalked me everywhere I went, they began to avoid me. Some became angry at me for engaging him, but they didn't understand how vicious he became when he was ignored.

He began saying that I had never been to Elan, which was stupid considering I had pictures of myself in front of Elan 7 and Elan 3, with Joe Peterson. He would have been easy to ignore if people didn't begin to believe him.

On every website there are trolls. Most people say things to each other on the internet that they wouldn't say to their face, but the trolls say things they wouldn't dare say for fear of being punched in the face. Of all the things that make the World Wide Web unpleasant, they irked me most.

None-Ya is a particularly nasty troll. He claimed that he didn't use his real name on the internet because he feared for his family, which was probably true, but it wasn't because of anything he was doing right. He was a coward and bully. He feared justice. None-Ya took Danny's side and began calling me a faggot and making jokes about me getting raped as a child.

"It's good I don't know who you are." I wrote. "Because if I did I would come to your house and shove that keyboard down your throat."

None-Ya used the next troll tactic, played the victim, and accused me of being an internet bully. "You threatened to stab Danny to death."

"You bet I did. He said he was coming to my house, so he threatened me first. He would only show up at my door for two reasons. If he wanted to die or if he wanted to kill me."

There were some Fornits members who believed None-Ya was a fake profile, or what they call, "a sock puppet," and there were some who didn't, but both sides were horrified by his behavior. I believed it because he went from being Danny's mortal enemy, to telling child rape jokes for him because he didn't believe I went to Elan. It didn't make sense.

In private messages members from both sides said they were tired of Fornits and didn't like it anymore. Most members visited rarely because it had become the Danny and Wayne Show. It was boring. I tried to stay away, but Danny's attacks warranted some participation.

I concentrated on the discussion about Gerald Davidson. So far we had connected him to the Human Potential Movement and its members, but it became hot when Jeff Wimbelton sent me a private message.

#

Jeff Wimbelton disappeared after Elan closed, and people said he was Gzasmyhero, but I had no idea who anyone really was. I saw the red light on my Facebook private message box, clicked on it and was happy to see it was from him.

In the message he had a quoted text from an old article:

"The Nixon Administration was, at one time, putting together a program for detaining youngsters who showed a tendency toward violence in "concentration" camps. According to the Washington Post, the plan was authored by Dr. Arnold Hutschnecker. Health, Education and Welfare Secretary Robert Finch was told by John Erlichman, Chief of Staff for the Nixon White House, to implement the program. He proposed the screening of children of six years of age for tendencies toward criminality. Those who failed these tests were to be destined to be sent to the camps. The program was never implemented."

"Michael Skakel wasn't talking out of his ass when he said Elan was a concentration camp for children." Jeff wrote. "DuPont worked for Nixon too."

It was compelling. "Makes you wonder who else was working for Nixon."

"Mitt Romney's father worked for Nixon."

Mitt Romney's father advised him to get a law degree at the same time as his business degree, in a new joint class that enrolled only fifteen students. He graduated in 1975, so he attended during the time thought reform and behavior modification were being studied. It would have been a small coincident if not for Romney's connections to the industry.

Romney was connected to Straight Inc. through Mel Sembler, which began with DuPont, who worked for Nixon. He was connected to WWASPS through his staffer, Robert Lichfield, and Aspen Education Group through Bain Capital. His involvement looked more like insider trading to me.

Matt got it right. "Who else to run the show than a Harvard businessman?"

Liz asked, "How much interest does Bain capital have in autism?"

"They have a partner who sits on the board of Autism Speaks."

I had already looked into other corporations Bain owned, and what their partners were doing. It was a lot of reading, but I was trapped in the house because of agoraphobia. After a few days I had found nothing, so I concentrated on other things.

"This guy is interesting."

"Who?"

Stanley Milgram went to Harvard, and his career was defined in the area of obedience to authority, which became the title of his book. He conducted the renowned experiments in which a doctor convinced people to continually shock a person though they were screaming in pain. Although the screamers were actors, the person pressing the button didn't know that and continued at the doctor's prompt.

"I remember him from the Synanon blog." I logged on and found the site. Then, the page. "Right here." I moved over so Liz could see.

"The American Association for the Advancement of Science awarded Milgram for his life's work in the area of obedience. One of his biggest fans was Charles Dederich."

XI

The information about the Nixon administration's plan to build concentration camps for kids raised some interest on Fornits. People joined in the discussion. I posted everything I could find on Larry brilliant, then a snippet from Doctor Arnold Hutschnecker's obituary.

"...who for many years served as Richard M. Nixon's psychotherapist and once said that Nixon "didn't have a serious psychiatric diagnosis" but had "a good portion of neurotic symptoms," died on a Thursday at his home in Sherman, Connecticut at the age of 102."

"Sherman is just a stone's throw from New Milford, where my doctor, M. Scott Peck lived. They had to know each other."

A member of the group with the username, Inculcated, wrote, "Not to come off all COINTELPRO or anything, but what is the working theory here?

"That Elan was an experiment."

Paul St. John said, "That's the thing that keeps coming back to me about it... the thing that I think may make it different.. like an incomplete idea judge floating 'round in my mind - never becoming anything, but never going away either. I have been suspicious about this for some time, but didn't want to state it, 'til I could figure out more... To be honest, I am not even sure why I think it.. I only know that something is missing from the puzzle, and that I think that this may be it. My "feeling", or "sense" for lack of a better term, is that it, at least, started out as an experiment, and then once it was in place, continued on, as a profitable "school", as it was there, so why not make money on it, and keep it going? My mind just keeps giving Elan importance, like there is a mystery there, with a very important conclusion.. One way or another, I may be wrong, but I know that my mind is doing this for a reason."

\#

Straight Inc. began as the Seed, which was formed by Art Barker, and like Joe Ricci, Art swore his form of therapy didn't come from Synanon, but it did. There was no mistaking it. Art was out of work and living of a friend's houseboat, when Robert DuPont gave him 1.8 million dollars to fund a treatment program for young adults.

Robert DuPont earned his M.D at Harvard in 1963, and continued his studies there and at the National Institutes of Health. According to a blog called, The Straights, " Robert L. DuPont, Jr., MD is the founding director of the National Institute on Drug Abuse (NIDA) and was also the second White House Drug Czar. While director of NIDA he administered funds for an experimental, juvenile drug rehabilitation program in Fort Lauderdale, Florida called The Seed."

I looked up from the computer, and said to Liz, "If they keep saying, "experimental," I'm going to start to think this was an experiment."

"That's exactly what it looks like."

"That's actually pretty cool."

She laughed.

"No, I'm serious. How many people can say they were actually brainwashed?"

"Is that what you think they did? Brainwashed you, I mean?"

"It's what they say."

"Who?"

I pointed to the computer screen. "The government."

"Despite the warnings of so many other notables, despite Art Barker's total lack of credentials and less than admirable past, The Seed received a $1.8 million U.S. government grant from the National Institute on Drug Abuse (NIDA) soon after it opened. And the grant had been administered by the founding director of NIDA who also happened to be the second White House Drug Czar-Robert DuPont. By 1975 Barker had opened four expansion Seeds, but in 1974 both houses of the US Congress had investigated The Seed and produced critical reports with the US Senate likening Barker's methods to the brainwashing methods employed on American POWs by North Korean Communists."

#

I believed that Elan was trying to use brainwashing to cure sociopaths. It would have explained why there were so many murderers in my house. But I was also convinced they were trying to create sociopathic behavior. Matt thought that was unlikely—Liz didn't.

"Robert Hyde wanted to develop a drug that caused schizophrenia." She said.

"What kind of monster would want to create something like that?"

"Dude gave LSD to mentally ill kids. He was involved with the CIA and MKUltra."

"Let me guess." I paused for effect. "He went to Harvard."

"Bingo."

Harvard was a common theme, but connections to each other and to the Human Potential Movement were beginning to mount. If we can put a man in the gas chamber based on circumstantial evidence, why can't we suppose on it?

Werner Erhard was interested in Synanon and the game, and the idea of using behavior modification to unleash talent and potential was interesting. It wasn't what Elan was doing to us. If someone wanted to explore my potential they would have first needed to get me as far away from Elan as possible.

Liz considered whether they were studying both unleashing and suppressing sociopathic personalities. A resident who was supposed to go on and kill more children left Elan and never got in any real trouble again, but the one who had never done drugs or been in trouble with the law was in prison for arson and addicted shortly after leaving.

"So, this guy Pat was a serial killer?"

"He talked about molesting and killing an eight year old kid like he was telling us how to change a flat tire."

"What about you?" She sat. "What did Doctor Peck say about you?"

"My mother said he was afraid of me."

"Really?"

Mom didn't explain why my doctor was afraid of me, but my father explained his part, which was he had no idea what Doctor Peck was talking about, and assumed he was doing the right thing.

It didn't make sense that anyone would be afraid of me when I was fourteen years old because I was shy and withdrawn. I was afraid all the time and mostly scared that people would find out I was crazy. But I wasn't bad crazy. I was not an abuser. I had a normal amount of physical altercations for a kid growing up in East New York, Brooklyn. I wasn't like the people who enjoyed hurting people.

"Peck probably believed I was a serial killer, or maybe he was just a greedy fuck getting paid for sending kids to programs."

It should have been long enough after thirty years to let go, and people asked all the time why there are a few Elan survivors who can't, but I didn't answer. How could we feel after Elan closed their doors, and no one was prosecuted? No one ever investigated them for sexual abuse though others told stories much like mine—that they were singled out for it, and it happened only once.

No one said anything negative about Elan aside from a few survivors who spoke about their experience there publicly. In the 1970s there were outspoken opponents of behavior modification interested in the rights of mentally ill kids, but they disappeared over the years.

"Who the fuck started sending mentally ill kids to Elan in the seventies?"

That was the question. Who gave the Maine department of health permission to use the game on kids who drifted in and out of reality? Who gave them permission to use an experimental treatment on children who had severe mental illness?

"Someone had to have given that person permission." Liz said.

"And, someone who gave him permission to grant it. And, somewhere in there, a panel of intellectual douchebags, and a few of those will be from Harvard."

#

Doctor Robert W. Hyde experimented on mentally ill kids with the blessing and money of the CIA, then went on to become a researcher for Harvard at a hospital now called the Massachusetts Mental Health Center, known for ties to the CIA. A congressional committee concluded that dozens of institutions had been involved in CIA experiments, and many had never been identified.

"Maybe their records blew up in a fire." I said.

Matt laughed. "Imagine what they destroyed."

Senator Frank Church said the CIA destroyed most of the drug and psychological evidence when word of the program's funding came to light. Were Elan, Seed or Straight Inc. records destroyed?

"I wouldn't be surprised." Matt said.

"What if they were isolating houses, like mine, and running experiments?"

"That I would believe. The CIA not so much."

"Skakel called it a concentration camp for kids. The Kennedy family was all up in the human potential movement." I paused. "It makes you wonder what they were thinking by sending him to Elan."

"Why would Rushton Skakel send him to a place that would beat a confession out of him?"

"Because he didn't do it." Matt didn't respond, so I continued. "He knew there was no physical evidence that could tie it to him, so a false confession after a beating would mean nothing."

"Until his murder trial."

"Rush would have kept the guilty son close to him, like he did. I'm convinced Tommy did it, and Mike got shafted by his family again."

"I don't know about that. The only ones who really know are them."

"Those Kennedys are bad news."

"They're bad luck."

\#

My brother signed a piece of paper with the landlord in October, ending his control of the lease. My father drove him, and his friend saw the document. We couldn't prove that, so Liz searched the internet and found a New York rent regulations guide. She found the laws governing succession of the lease. According to it we were covered. We had been living there for over a year and were disabled. The eviction notice soon followed.

"This is ridiculous." I said. "He can't possibly win this."

"We need a lawyer."

In the Queens civil court there is a Legal Aid office that can only take twenty new cases a day, so people line up early and it gets contentious as the time arrives to be on the short list. Liz and I tried twice and were pushed out of line both times. It felt like they were throwing scraps to a pack of dogs, and because it was a matter of survival the crowd acted accordingly.

"I'm too old for this. Let's talk to our councilman."

Liz was doubtful that anyone was going to help us because New York's war on the poor was vicious. Any money we had was gone in short time. The price of food and housing left us broke and fighting off hunger at the end of every month. They wanted us gone and budget cuts were the way to achieve that.

\#

Ted Kaczynski was also known as the Unabomber. His story is well known, but his brother brought the question that no one bothered to answer. "Was my brother, Ted Kaczynski (AKA "the Unabomber"), a sort of "Manchurian candidate" - programmed to kill by our government in a CIA-funded thought-control experiment gone awry?"

Many people considered it absurd, but many though otherwise. I didn't believe it was true, but I saw Harvard was involved and was open to any argument. Who knew the results of their experiments, and what they were capable of?

"Makes you wonder about Jimmy Shiplett though." Matt said. "Ken Zaretsky handed him a gun and sent him to the sheriff's station to get his girlfriend out."

"Because he was told to do it. Who goes to a place full of men with guns waiving a pistol?"

"He wasn't that drunk."

The conversation on Fornits asked if maybe Jared Loughner, the Arizona gunman who had killed six people, may have been in a program, and a possible Manchurian candidate. He had been in a residential treatment center which was not being revealed, and the one most likely program was Teen Challenge.

Representative Gabrielle Giffords was shot in the head, but lived and got the majority of the press. "I wonder if the judge who was killed was a Teen Challenge supporter."

"I wonder if Gabrielle Giffords was." Someone said.

#

Matthew Israel founded the Judge Rottenberg Center and studied under B.F. Skinner at Harvard. He called behavioral psychology, "experimental science," and used beatings and torture on autistic and mentally ill kids. His center was the focus of a recent lawsuit and was under fire for horrible abuses. Some said their kids did well after going there, but the horror stories were very Elan-like.

"Harvard, eh?" Liz said.

"Yup."

#

Fornits poster with the screen name Ursus had commented on the article about Israel and the Rotenberg Center years earlier.

Ursus 08/25/2007 12:15 AM

Re. the evolution of JRC from Skinner: Something about that time, I'm not sure what it was, created a hotbed for these types of places. There were a lot of new ideas floating around about the human psyche, and people tried mucking around with those ideas, for whatever reasons... perhaps some of them were even good-intentioned. I guess some people thought they could apply these ideas to solving some of the "problems of the day," e.g., straightening up the "errant and wayward youth" and turning them into productive citizens. It would seem that the idea that one's teenage years are, by definition, turbulent times fraught with stress and filled with a modicum of experimentation, had not yet been accepted as not necessarily a bad thing. Apparently it still isn't. ...Matthew Israel appears to have escaped close scrutiny of his methods and ideology since he focused on a small subset of youth, namely, self-abusing and mentally disturbed individuals whose parents felt they had no other alternative. His target clientele in the early days weren't exactly able to speak for themselves. Now that the Judge Rotenberg Center has started to target more mainstream malcontents, be it for reasons of greed or myopia, we are starting to hear stories of what life is really like there. May the sunlight of this current exposure prove to be the requisite disinfectant needed to put these atavistic barbaric cruelties to rest.

#

"Keep pounding away at this." Matt said. "You're really onto something."

Matt wasn't convinced of my ideas about government involvement in experimentation, but was intrigued.. I had mentioned the fact Davidson was unpublished a few times, but Matt didn't understand what my wife did about academics. She asked me, so I asked Matt.

"How did an unpublished nobody get to testify before congress?" Why didn't he publish after? Or, along the way since? Hey, how about something other than Elan? "

"That is very intriguing."

"Well, I can't prove Gerald Davidson was working for the government, and there's nothing else available on him, so I'm on to something else."

"What's that?"

"There's a guy on an Elan Facebook group named Juan Ferrerya who went to Elan, and says he opened a similar program in Argentina."

"Seriously?"

"Uh-huh, and what's more, is he says he wants to reopen the Poland Springs campus."

XII

The internet changed the world by giving a voice to anyone with a computer and connection, but it also opened them to predators. I found out right away that Danny had sent private messages to my friends and family, and attacked anyone who supported my book, but he went further by creating profiles with fake names, and telling people they were friends of his, and that I had never gone to Elan. He told them that he and a group of friends had my ISP and enough evidence to present a case to a grand jury. Some people believed him.

With my brother gone, we were relaxed but broke. I slept well for the first time in a year, but my OCD was as bad as it had ever been, so it was mostly unrestful. Physically, I was a mess. I woke with pain every morning and couldn't breathe until after a cup of tea or coffee. Mentally, I was sharp, but physically I felt old.

I had known about Juan Ferrerya for weeks, and was ready for him when he surfaced because I gathered information on him from two fake profiles in a pro-Elan group on Facebook, He commented on a discussion about the Elan campus being for sale. Everyone said they wanted to buy the property and open something, but they were mostly kidding around. Juan was serious when he said he intended to buy it and reopen Elan, and said he would need help.

"This is crazy. Who the fuck would want to reopen that place?"

Liz handed me her laptop. "Read what he has to say about Joe Ricci on the Elan Alum site."

"I don't have my glasses. What does it say?"

"You can read the whole thing later, but I'll tell you this, he says Joe was an angel from heaven and that he opened a similar program in Argentina."

I went to find my glasses.

#

The first thing I found on Juan Ferreira was that he used a different spelling for his professional profile than his Facebook page. It was spelled, Ferrerya, there. Suspicion set in right away. I was nice to him in an e-mail, so he wrote back and asked why people would say negative things about his program.

"I don't know what to say."

Liz screwed her face up, and then said, "Tell him you want to open one of those soft approach programs that are doing so well, and you'll help him do it."

"There's big money in that. Rich people don't want their kids abused."

"That's a good idea."

He wrote back and said he wanted to stay in touch, and found the proposal intriguing. I was on the inside with the man who wanted to reopen the place of our nightmares. I only shared that with three people, but that was one person too many. One commented on Fornits about Juan and Danny, so Juan blocked me on Facebook and ceased all contact.

"That's fucked up." Liz said.

"Why would someone who went through that place torpedo me?"

She could see the disappointment I was going through. "Do that marine thing. Improvise, adapt and overcome."

"Yeah, I guess....But I fucking had him...."

"I'm sorry."

I improvised.

#

I had a dream once that God chose me to speak to the world and tell them the secret to happiness. I followed God through the rest of the dream and asked what I should say because I didn't know the secret to happiness, and was getting nervous as the time to announce it drew near. He told me I would know when the time came.

As the time to speak grew near I became afraid, but when I was escorted out onto a balcony I began to panic. The streets were crowded and there were people on the roofs and in windows. Some sat or hung from tree branches. I still had no idea what to say.

I looked at God, who nodded to me and said, "Go ahead."

I stepped up to the microphone and said, "Stay away from negative people."

They loved it. The cheers went on for five minutes.

"You need to do that on the internet." God said.

#

"Yeah."

Liz looked up from her book. "What?"

"That whole, staying away from negative people, thing. I need to apply it to the internet."

"That's probably a good idea."

I quit every troubled teen group and unfriended program people. The ones I kept interacted with me every day and had become friends. Danny became more and more vicious as I distanced myself, but saw I was determined not to respond and stopped provoking me.

"He's over on Orange Papers being Danny." Matt said.

"What's Orange Papers?"

"It's an anti AA site. A lot of Stinkin Thinkin people go there now."

"Maybe I'll check it out. Not say anything."

"Stay away from Bennison. You seem so much happier."

The news about Juan Ferrerya had Elan survivors upset, rightfully, but Juan didn't just block me and ignore me. He didn't speak on the subject of Elan again, I knew because I was still in his group under another fake profile. His silence convinced me that he had the intention of doing it, but I had nothing to base that on.

"Hammer away at him." Matt said.

"With what?"

Danny solved that problem by starting a discussion on Fornits about Juan.

#

Most accept people at face value on the internet at first, but that is a mistake. The consequences are hardly ever serious, but the one time you meet a stalker it changes you. Trust on the internet is not a good idea, I know because I've been stalked by the best. I could see which fake profiles on Fornits were fake, and a lot of Elan posters could too. We knew Ruaraidh was Danny right away.

Ruaraidh, (Danny) accused me of creating Juan Ferrerya on Fornits and said there was no Elan clone in Argentina, but a member quoted his post and said that Juan was real and Ibicuy was real, and directed us to search for "program Ibicuy," in a Youtube search.

"Doesn't get realer than that." He said.

Ursus wrote. "Yep. Moreover, people have been posting about it here since 2007, possibly even earlier."

The filth Danny posted about me, and the fake friend profiles were being accepted. Some members told him they knew they were his, but he ignored them. However, there were people who believed what they saw, so I created fake profiles of my own.

I used fake profiles to make a mockery of sock puppetry, and Danny's attacks, but that ended when my reputation for having sock puppets blew up in my face. Ursus commented that it may actually be true that I created a fake Juan Ferrerya profile on Facebook.

In the next comment, Danny said he was coming to see me in New York City, so I responded that if he came to my door I would kill him. I wasn't lying. I didn't care what I had to do to say what Danny had been doing to me on the internet. Ursus quoted the threat and made a joke about a misused set of words, and I fell apart.

I signed out of the site and turned off the computer, then stared at the blank screen for twenty minutes. That's too long a time for me to be quiet, so Liz came in from the living room and asked me what was wrong.

"It's been so long they forgot who the victim is here. I wouldn't care, but they've begun to attack me. If someone disagrees with me they go to Fornits to provoke him into attacking me." I slammed my hand down on the desk. "That son of a bitch raped me!"

She put her hand on mine.

#

Our first day of Queens County housing court started in a line hundreds of people long. It was cold and the wind was fierce. When that was over, we sat and waited in the hallway outside the courtroom six hours for our names to be called. When they called us, we asked for time to get a lawyer, and were given two weeks.

"That's not enough time."

I shrugged. "The law is clear. Why don't we just represent ourselves?"

"Why don't you ask Krista for help? It 'is' Catholic Charities."

"That's not a bad idea."

"Uh-huh, and a week from now you'll be saying it was your idea."

"I was just thinking of that."

She smirked. "Let's get out of here."

#

We arrived home to a ringing phone. I knew it was Matt. "Hi Matt."

"How did you know it was me?"

"I don't know. What's up?"

In my half day away from the internet, someone had dug up Juan Ferrerya's information on professional sites and said it didn't make sense for someone to create a fake profile. Danny fired back, accusing the poster of being me.

"Why doesn't anyone defend me?"

"They're afraid of him." He said.

When I first put the book up they all loved me, but some grew tired of the bickering and distanced themselves from me, but until I watched that discussion I hadn't realized that no one defended me anymore.

I said to Matt. "It's the same as it was in Elan. They're happy it's me and not them."

"I don't know about that."

"Well I do, and some day I'm going to add to this freak show by killing myself if someone doesn't get this man off of me." I told him about the e-mails and phone calls, and the eventual dead-ends. No one would stop him, and it was overwhelming. "I can't live like this. He knows about my OCD and uses it against me. He's sick."

"There's no doubt about that, Bennison is a sick motherfucker. He'll find what hurts you and use it."

"But what can I do. He's turned Fornits into Elan. He parades me in front of everyone and attacks me. Then turns everyone against me. And, just like in Elan, people don't dare go against him. This is like being raped all over again."

"The world would be a better place if Bennison wasn't dancing on it. We need you around to finish the story."

"At times the story still feels like a suicide note." I said. "I'm a little afraid of the end."

That night the news came to me that Danny and his fake profiles had been banned from Facebook. We had a party.

\#

The day Elan closed was nothing compared to Danny's Facebook sendoff. Only seven people attended, but they were old friends I hadn't seen online for a long time. They thanked me for my book, and Patrick said something about it helping close down Elan.

"All I did was give you guys Bennison. Honestly, that's good enough for me."

I posted everything I had on Juan Ferrerya, and we swore that he would never reopen Elan. I stayed when everyone left to sleep, then visited a few groups, and enjoyed my first night on Facebook without Danny Bennison.

I received a flood of private messages that night and found the worst one. It stated that Danny still had one profile by the name of, Leeroy Strong who was still on survivor sites defending, "his good pal, Danny."

"He spelled Leroy wrong."

Matt laughed. "He spelled Isaac wrong too. That's how everyone knew that was him."

"He's on the Jani Foundation wall spewing his garbage. How could he use a mentally ill or autistic kid to get to me?"

"If you remember, this is the guy who tried to push Lee to kill herself. He's a sick sadistic predator. He never changed."

"Well, we need to hammer on "Leeroy," and let Facebook know he has a fake proxy and another account."

"Cool."

"Hey, other than that, we kicked his fucking ass off of Facebook."

"Isn't it great?"

I had posted on Fornits early on asking Danny to stop harassing and threatening women. When Elan first closed, he knew that would hurt me more than an attack on me, so, every day one woman or another posted about his threats. I told him that I would take the book down and leave all groups, and leave him alone, but he declined. He enjoyed the circus he created, but the culmination of reports to Facebook grew until they had to ban him.

Later that night, I got news that the Elan property had been sold, and the man who had bought it was a veterinarian. The person who told me said we should look into his affiliations with Sharon Terry, and the racetrack.

I wrote back. "I'm on it, but let's keep this between us for now, huh?"

He replied with a confirmation.

#

Juan was no longer a threat to reopen Elan, but the thread Danny started took an ugly turn when the comments on the youtube videos about Ibucuy were translated. It was clear that Juan took Elan to South America. He spoke highly of his program in public, but the comments told another story. The sickness was taking lives all over the world.

The commenters spoke of suicide after suicide. One parent said her son killed himself after he left Ibucuy. Another said her son lived, but when he came home from Ibucuy, she didn't recognize him. Matt and I discussed what to do, and couldn't come up with a plan better than hammering away at him.

""And while we're doing that we can check into the new owner of Poland Springs."

"I have a court date tomorrow and I have to get to my therapist, but I'm on this Kinney guy tomorrow morning."

"Hey, good luck with that."

"I don't need luck. I need a lease in my name."

"Are you sure about succession?"

"Yeah, it has three categories and I fall under all of them. What could be up for interpretation?"

"Well, be careful."

"Oh, I'm being very careful. His lawyer is too confident."

#

On February 24th, 2012, I posted a question to Fornits. "Who is Stephen J. Kinney the new owner of the Elan Poland campus?" It was sure Danny was still trying to gain favor from someone in Poland immediately.

"Juan Ferreira is not trying to reopen Elan, that's stupid."

"I know. Juan was a shiny object. This guy bought the property."

And it continued.

XIII

When Danny was gone from Facebook and my brother from the apartment, I was able to get consecutive night's sleep for the first time in a year. Tension worked itself away. After the anger and fear were gone, I was hungry. For the first time since arriving in New York, Liz and I explored the neighborhood for food.

The first thing I notice when I get somewhere new and drop my bags is the crows. If there are none I notice that. The first thing I noticed when we arrived in Queens is that there were none, and it gave me a deep foreboding. People saw crows as an ominous sign, but I knew better. Life isn't right without them.

Crows are among the world's smartest animals. They make and use tools, recognize faces and exhibit emotion. They grieve as a group by gathering in closely bunched trees, screeching as loud as they can. Liz and I witnessed it one day. I wanted to be a crow after that, and joined their Facebook group.

The morning after Danny's farewell party from Facebook, a crow landed in a small tree on 43rd Street and looked at me like he knew me. I said, "Hi," and he chipped at me. His chirp was not melodious, and sounded more like a chip.

#

Our second trip to housing court was less painful. The temperature was better and the wind less fierce. We arrived later to a much shorter line. The judge didn't enter the courtroom until almost ten o'clock the first trip, so there was no reason to get there at eight thirty.

Liz was ready. She had a solid case that Kenny and the landlord were working together to harass us out of the apartment, and evidence that they both broke the law. I had a printed copy of the New York City housing law that conceded my succession rights. We felt confident.

It felt wrong when we entered the court room and got worse as it went along. The first thing we were told is that the hearing wasn't a holdover, which I didn't understand. When I asked, the woman said the hearing was to determine if we owed the money. I told her we didn't deny owing the money.

"The first thing I'd like to ask you people to do is stop calling this nonpayment. That's not true. We offered him the rent and he said he doesn't have to accept it."

The judge and clerk didn't look like they cared. No one flinched, so I didn't trust anything. We were the only ones in the courtroom. That's never good.

We told our story, and they told theirs, and it was over. I told the judge that Catholic Charities was going to help us because we proved the back rent was stolen from us by my brother, but I needed the lease in my name to ensure they weren't throwing away their money. The judge said that it wasn't an issue for that court. The clerk said we would receive a decision in five days by post, and we headed home.

Outside, I said, "This feels wrong."

Liz looked surprised. "What do you mean? I thought the judged liked us. He said we owe the money, which means he's saying we're the tenants."

"Why were we the only ones in that courtroom?"

Her look turned to confusion for a second, then recognition. She knew what I was going to say. I didn't like to ruin her sense of comfort, but it was better than false hope. We had been to housing court more than once, and it was a lesson that almost destroyed us.

"That felt a lot like Patterson."

She frowned. "It did, didn't it?"

"We need to get a lawyer."

#

There are people you see and communicate with every day, but if they're not your Facebook friend they feel like complete strangers. It's hard to understand, but true, my internet friends had become my real friends. We found places to be ourselves and share our dreams and secrets, away from the ridicule of the ones who loved us.

When we arrived home and I had tea I went to Facebook, but it was quiet. That was good because it gave me less distraction from looking into Stephen Kinney, the new owner of, 70 Number Five Road. People weren't convinced he was connected to program people. One said he might be opening a place for animals.

"That's too steep a grade. Most of the property isn't fit for animals." Matt said. "And the buildings all have to come down. They're unsafe."

I cradled the phone between my ear and shoulder, checked my computer. "I have an article with Kinney and race horses, but haven't read it yet."

"Interesting."

"Very."

I read the article as Matt caught me up on Danny's abuses on Orange Papers forum. The organization Kinney was with was against horse racing, and thought it was inhumane. The first thing that I considered was they might be trying to sway people into being sympathetic to Sharon Terry's hope for a casino gambling license.

Matt confirmed my suspicion. "I wonder if gaming tables might be the solution."

"That's what I was just thinking."

#

My thread on Fornits got ugly quickly. Danny always accused the poster called, Muppeteer, of being me, but it wasn't. Muppeteer and I discussed whether Juan Ferrerya might still be involved, but decided he was a small part of the equation if he was, and concentrated on Stephen Kinney.

I found an article linking him to a horse owner in Maine who had lost his medical license for drug use The Bangor Times referenced to Steve Kinney as a trainer of Morgan horses owned by Jeff Violette of Bucksport, Maine.

"Now we're getting somewhere."

Liz was set up in the living room with her laptop, and I at the personal computer, by the side of the bed, so we could see each other through the doorway. We needed to be in eye contact when we researched together because my eyes were better than my ears.

"This isn't much." She said.

"Think about it. He's a horse owner and the race track owner is the most famous drug program owner in the world." I stood. "He's also known as a dirty dealer, and a crook." I stopped in the doorway. "If I was him and my medical license was in danger, I would have gone straight to Joe Ricci."

She nodded. "Me too."

The organization Steve Kinney belonged to was the Animal Refuge League of Portland, and the members were rich. The first member was a drunken driving lawyer, so I posted a link to his website on Fornits, and wrote, "Danny could certainly be involved with this guy."

The second member I checked out worked for UBS, which linked him to Bain Capital and Mitt Romney, but that was a wide field of association. Liz said that we needed a direct link to a program like WWASPS or Aspen Education. I found it on my next search.

"Alyssa Hemingway, Hyde School. Hyde Foundation. This is the chick."

Liz found her on the laptop. She looked up. "You got it."

#

If you post a lot of repetitive information into a discussion on the internet with the purpose of getting people to give up reading it in frustration, that is called, "Flooding." I know because I had been banned for it twice. People complained, but I explained that when I did it, Danny became angry and gave himself away. I had gotten his fake profiles to slip up and admit they were him four times.

Danny unleashed on the Stephen Kinney discussion with vulgar posts from an off-topic thread about his nieces. Many thought Danny started the off-topic discussion, but I didn't believe it. I was sure it was another of Elan's nasty trolls, but when he posted it over and over in the threads about Elan's new owner, I was no longer convinced.

I called Matt. "Why the fuck would he repost that shit?"

"Better question is, why is he flooding that discussion? All he's doing now is showing that you're on to something."

"With None Ya right by his side, telling faggot and baby rape jokes. Are you sure it's not Danny?"

"No…Simply, no."

"He created his own enemy so he could find out what people know about him."

"That would be one hell of a trick, and I won't say it's impossible. I can't believe the shit he's posting."

\#

I finally wrote one long post and put it in the Stephen Kinney discussion:

"I know some of you people don't like me, and hate Elan survivors in particular, but you guys don't get it. I hear that we're off the wall, and the worst trolls and all that,"

"Imagine how Straighlings would act if Miller Newton or Mel Sembler were here doing to them what Danny is doing to us."

"I didn't mind your anger. But None Ya, if you're not Danny, you need to do something. If someone thought I was him, I'd turn this computer off and seriously consider my life."

"I never said I had anything to do with closing Elan. I've always said I helped the people who did, and I gave them Danny Bennison."

"You loved me when my book came out, but none of you defended me when that horrible guy Eric slayed it with lies. You don't say anything when Danny uses his sock puppets to attack me. You've joined in on the jokes."

"Danny Bennison beat, raped and tortured me in 1978, at the Elan School."

"That's all I have left to say, other than trying to keep Hyde from reopening Elan. If you remember, the Gordon kid was sent there when they closed."

#

Muppeteer was on the same page and posed the question, "What if they're trying to open a Hyde school?"

"My thoughts exactly."

Ursus quoted the information I posted about Alyssa Hemingway and said, "Hyde School CFO Alyssa Hemingway is also listed in the Hyde Faculty and Staff thread, in addition to being quoted in the thread re. Some proposed construction: NEW DORM to be razed; $3M "New Dorm II" to be built in Bath."

"Thank you."

Muppeteer went to check out Alyssa, I went after the construction deal. Giving sweetheart deals to your friends in the construction business is an age old scam and Hyde was paying for theirs with foundation money. I had a good feeling there was something there, which Ursus confirmed with a story that questioned Hyde's over-construction, and blamed them for flooding caused by it.

"This is great. Thank you."

I read the article and went back the Fornits and said, "So, they're creating work at the tax payer's expense? Bunch of those animal rescue people are in construction. It's worth looking into."

I found an animal rescue board member who was a lawyer, and served the needs of the construction industry. "Cozy up there in Maine."

"Oh, yeah."

#

There was an allegation that Hyde attempted to cover up a gang rape, followed by supporting comments. I had read enough about Hyde to know the Game. I quoted and posted two comments about the gang rape and Duncan McCrann, and then the link and part of a sports article someone dropped in my Elan group.

"With one-third of the season still remaining for most teams, only three unbeaten boys' clubs remain in the entire state. All are in Western Maine: Falmouth in Class B, Dirigo in Class C and Hyde in Class D. Hyde's first-year coach is Peter Rowe, a Livermore Falls native and longtime leader of the program at Elan School in Poland Spring, which closed its doors in April 2011."

XIV

The court decision arrived after three days and demanded that we pay the amount of rent we were prepared to pay, but made no mention of the lease being put in our name. Catholic Charities couldn't get us any money without a lease.

"This doesn't help us one bit." I said.

"What can we do?"

"Wait till he takes us back to court and file a counter suit. They're not going to throw two disabled people in the street."

"Yeah. I believed that before Patterson."

This time it was Liz who brought up Patterson, and our introduction to small town justice. When the landlord learned I was unable to work after my fall on the ice in 2008, he came to the cabin and told Liz that my injury was no excuse to fall behind with the rent, and he expected it on the first.

"Why don't you get the fuck out of my living room?" I said. "I have no intention of paying you because this is your fault."

Liz tried to stop me. "Wayne—"

The rent was paid, and what he was demanding wasn't due for two weeks. He had come to start a fight, and he knew that the tone of voice he used with her would start one, so I came out swinging.

I said to Liz, "Fuck that, he came here for a fight." Then, I said to him, "And you, I asked to leave."

"This is my property—"

I cut him off. "Not until you throw me out it isn't. And this cabin isn't legal. I'll sue for my money back. All of it."

He left, and then came back with his wife when they read my letter. We had all the violations on the property, the illegal alterations, and a very questionable tax assessment that we believed was a mistake. It wasn't. The assessment was a crime between the landlord and his friends with the assessor's office. I told him I would see him in court.

The judge was nice when the room was full of people and gave us two weeks to find a lawyer, but when we returned and the lawyer didn't show up, he was mean, and ordered me to go forward without a lawyer. He told me to shut up three times, and ordered us out. He also ruled that we owed Makram Matta $1,000 when it was the other way around. He owed us money.

He told me to shut up when I brought up the fact that the cabin was illegal, and when I said that Mister Matta was cheating the town with the assessor, and that the insurance company had never been to the property to do an assessment he screamed. By that time we knew he was in on it. That was confirmed when I went to the tax collector's office and the judge was sitting behind the desk in the middle of a telephone call.

Small town justice is a bitch. But it was a small part of a large world that had no use for us anymore. We took the room with my brother with the assumption that there were people who fought for the poor in New York City, but it was an understaffed and overburdened system. We were afraid.

"I don't like this one bit."

I didn't either.

#

My 48th birthday was the best of my life. Elan announced they were closing that day and the world celebrated all night long on the day I was born. Matt, Mark and I spent the night calling and messaging each other. I got private messages from Elan survivors that brought tears to my eyes.

My 49th birthday was approaching and I was tired. That was all, after the nightmare of Danny and Kenny's abuse—I was tired. 50 was the age we chose for suicide when we were kids.

Richie Morrison used to say, "At fifty you take the pill." My father reminded him on his 60th birthday.

I was one year shy, but I had a purpose in life at forty nine years old. I wanted to live to finish my story. I wanted to fulfill my promise to tell all survivors' stories and be part of the solution, but didn't have the temper to advocate on the internet.

"You're a writer." Matt laughed. "Write."

It sounds easy enough the 300,000 times you say it to yourself, and just as easy when someone else tells you, but every once in a while you hear it. That day, I heard it. Matt told me he was going to be working a lot, which was fine because he was my favorite waste of time, and I needed to tell the story. The book about the book.

I told him about it.

"It's a good story." He said.

I reminded him I had few minutes left on my phone. "I have to send a money order to a girl from the Jani Foundation. I need them to call her."

"Alright. I gotta go anyway. I'm approaching a place where I lose my signal."

"Be good brother."

"Peace."

#

The internet brings you daily heartbreak and horror. Abused kids, animals and housewives, cancer and oppression bombard social networks. Debates rage all day and night across barriers that were never there. Unlike mainstream media, there were inspirational and feel-good stories, but as good as most of it was, the negativity had worn me down.

We had gotten rid of the television years before because it was too much stimulation. Even if it was on low in the background it was too much for me. When the TV was on I had anxiety attacks, and when it wasn't, I didn't. We got rid of the TV and they stopped altogether.

The computer had the same stimulation, but it was obvious to me, and though I surrendered to it at times, I controlled it well. I learned my limitations and protected myself. Writing offline had no stimulation, so that was my objective.

They say to sit and stare at the screen until your eyes bleed if you can't write. I sat and stared at the computer for twelve hours a day for a week before I wrote anything. I took the rule very seriously. My books were selling in the hundreds every month, so there was an added reason to live. I had one story left to tell and was prepared to sit and stare at that computer screen until I died. Unfortunately, the computer died first.

My sister had given me an old laptop that didn't work well with the internet, but we hoped it would be good enough to download and use a writing program. The download took three hours at the library.

"I can do forty five minutes a day for Facebook and all that here at the library, because if I'm going to write this book that will be all the time I have for the internet."

"And, it's a reason to get out of the house."

"True."

"We need to get food, by the way." She pointed to the door.

"What do you want to get?"

"Let's go to the European butcher."

"Hot dogs."

#

The hot dogs at the European butcher were dark red and linked, which was what hot dogs looked like when I was a kid. The owner said they were red because she used real meat, and there was no doubt. We had them a few times a week. Our new interest outside the internet was food and we knew food. We did it well.

The world was in serious trouble in the real world too, but the impending feeling of doom was less. My OCD was crippling me with it, so I needed to retreat from my real friends and be with real live people. We joke about it until it happens.

In the real world people talk to each other, and my hearing is bad, so it's uncomfortable in that respect. They like to talk on the phone, but I talk over them because of my old ears, so I hate that. Tiring as it is, I like to type a response to something, and have a few seconds to deliver my words. It keeps things more courteous.

The real world has interesting people, and if you show an interest in them, they take a liking to you. We were very popular at the butchers, grocers, restaurants and spice stores. We asked questions and had long conversations with people from around the world. A store called, "Parrot," had a man from Israel at the register, a man from Lebanon in the meat department, and girls from Turkey and Romania. The owners were Greek and Romanian.

Outside, I stopped. "Are we the only country that doesn't get along with anyone?"

She laughed. "No. You still have that internet negativity in your head."

In the real world there isn't an abused kid or dog flashed before your eyes every five minutes. People know the horror exists and go about their lives, struggling to survive, and depressed by the futility of trying to do something about it. They survive better without the constant reminders.

\#

Susan Schofield had been suggested by a friend, so I sent her a friend request on Facebook and she accepted. It was a few days before I found out who she was, and that she had been on Oprah and 20/20 because of the struggle she had with her daughter. Before I knew who she was, she had asked me to be on her radio show.

I told the story of A Life Gone Awry, and connected behavior modification to Mitt Romney, Mel Sembler and Robert Lichfield. We talked about Miller Newton and Straight Inc. and WWASPS. Bain Capital and Aspen Education Group.

"This is a business."

The second time I was on her show, I thought I was ready to tell the story of being raped at Elan, but the idea that it was going out to real people hit me immediately. I stuttered and stammered and tripped over my own words. It was a bad idea.

"At least you said it." Liz said. "I'm proud of you."

\#

I sent Susan Schofield a private message and got the name of a girl who needed money, went to the post office, and sent it. As little or much as the money for the book was, I gave it to someone who needed it.

Liz was in the hospital that day, I know because when the marshal handed me the eviction notice as I got back to the house, I never felt so alone. No matter what direction our relationship was going to take, I still wanted to be with her.

I tucked the notice in my briefcase, went to bed and slept, and woke with the flu. I couldn't get any further than the bathroom for three days. There was no food and no phone, and Liz didn't come home.

On the fourth day I made it to court, filled out an order to show cause, and waited to speak to the judge. Again, the courtroom was empty. I didn't get to speak. I sat on the bench for two minutes, the bailiff asked me to step outside, and informed me that the judge rejected my order, and we had three days to move.

I called New York Hospital and found Liz. "They kept me for a few days and you don't have a phone. They're getting ready to release me today."

"I'll be right there."

I went to get my wife.

\#

Everywhere we went at the Queens courthouse was mobbed except the room we were denied our rights in. It was a back room, and Richie Morrison said it best when he said, "They can take you in the back room and shove a nightstick up your ass," because that was what happened to us there. It raped us both and left us with nothing but anger. The people we called and spoke to said it was unfortunate and told us to sue, but we would likely die before that happened.

"What are we going to do?" Liz was afraid. When she went into the hospital there was no indication that we were going to be evicted, and even an eviction gives ample time to move. She came out into a nightmare. We had no money and nowhere to go.

"We have my sister, my father and Susan Schofield, don't worry about it."

#

Al Dumont came to the rescue. When he heard we were in need, he gave us a place in Torrington, Connecticut. Al loved us because we were good tenants. We borrowed some money, rented a car, and fucked up a few credit cards, and landed in Torrington. As we moved, Liz and I planned to live apart for a few months, so after she was settled in, on May 5th, I jumped on a bus to Lebanon, Missouri, intent on writing the end of my memoirs.

I had started for Missouri once, planned it twice, and it didn't happen either time. The ticket was $168, and a friend needed someone to housesit and take care of his dogs. It was a thirty six hour trip, but I was ready for the real world. I started at a small depot in Torrington, and according to the schedule I was going to see a lot of the country.

"I've never traveled." I told her. "I feel like stretching my legs."

I got on the bus, and she watched until I was out of sight. I watched her until she was. I knew if she didn't follow me to Missouri I would be coming back, and Torrington would be the place I die, but I had four free months to write my book. It was all I had left to do.

I felt alone right away.

XV

If you want to see the real world close-up and personal, go Greyhound. The trip from Torrington to Hartford was a morning commuter bus. Though it was the first step, it didn't feel like the beginning of a thousand mile journey. I didn't feel like a traveler yet because my bus from Hartford to New York didn't leave for nearly eight hours.

My plan was to see Hartford and have lunch somewhere in the city, but the woman at the ticket window told me they don't check bags. I hadn't checked the website and assumed it. I was grounded, and not just in Hartford. With my duffle bag I couldn't enjoy any of my layovers.

The good news was that the bus depot had free wireless internet and electric outlets. The website didn't mention that the buses had been upgraded and the new ones had free wifi as well. My disappointment was quelled. I grabbed a table, bought a sandwich and signed into Facebook.

I let everyone know I was on the road and checked the news. Scientists announced on that day a device that can be integrated into a garment, which would monitor your heart and send health information to your Smartphone. That was as exciting as it got. The world was quiet. I went to Fornits, then Topix and every Elan discussion I could find, and they were dead.

There was no reason not to write, so I did for an hour at a time. It was a difficult trip to the bathroom with all my bags, so I turned off the new laptop and had a smoke in the same trip. People came and went, so when it was quiet I had three good writing sessions. None had anything to do with the memoir, but I had over 6,000 words.

It started with a whim. "Wouldn't it be cool to write an erotica in a public place? And from there it took off. I started with the Chinese girl in the corner, and threw in the Jewish girl and her boyfriend to my right. The black man with the tattoos was perfect.

The gay guy fucked it up because he was too fabulous to leave out and too fabulous to fit into the script. I was knocked out of my groove, so I went to have a cigarette. The bus to New York was about to arrive.

\#

The bus from Hartford to New York was crowded, loud, and angry. People complained that their layovers for food breaks were cut to five minute smoke breaks, and worst of all, the seating space was exaggerated. I had wifi and a plug, but there wasn't enough room to open my laptop. It ruined the mood.

The bus from New York to Newark was much less crowded, so I was able to sit sideways and open the laptop. I signed into wifi and announced my location to my friends on Facebook, and the world was good again. I wrote a 2,000 word press release for The Game as I made friends with the guy in front of me.

The young man in the seat in front of me had no luggage. His clothes were all in garbage bags, and Greyhound wouldn't let him keep them with baggage, so he had a seat to himself. I had one as well because the advantage to being big is people sit with smaller people before you. The drawback is getting on a bus with one person in each seat, and the look they all give you.

To add to the festivities, the driver announced that we could get off and have a cigarette at the Newark station before we continued on. The mood died again when we got off to smoke. There was a large group of people ready to board the bus.

One lady stubbed her cigarette out quickly and said, "I'm going to get my seat." She looked like she knew what she was doing, so I looked to find my seat already taken. "These people should not have been let on board until we reboarded." She said when she saw.

I went to have another cigarette and surrendered to the agony of the real world. I sat with a nice guy I had spoken to about hockey as we approached the station. The New Jersey Devils were playing the Philadelphia Flyers, and the crowd in the streets were wearing jerseys and razzing each other.

I surrendered and put the laptop away, and stored it overhead, and we sat in the dark sipping vodka and talking about hockey. The real world had its moments.

#

I slept until a Pennsylvania rest stop in the middle of nowhere, where I bought a pack of cigarettes for less than five dollars. "I feel like a kid again."

The saleslady laughed. "Where are you from?"

"New York City. These are twelve fifty there."

Everyone groaned, and I listened to three people tell me they thought it was bad where they were from. If you're from New York City, you're king of tax oppression on about any bus. A pint of whiskey was seventeen dollars. I got an earful for mentioning it.

From Pennsylvania to Cleveland we slept and I woke hungry, so I followed my nose. I smelled hamburgers, and found them right away. The lady was nice, and funny. She made me laugh, and I remember people who make me laugh, so I remember her well.

A handful of us had gravitated to each other, but at Cleveland some were going in another direction, and we felt loss. Some had exchanged numbers with them to stay in touch as we rode. We ate and drank coffee, and had fun. We loved Cleveland until we had to connect. The line had grown by so many people, that we were not going to get on the bus.

The end of the line feels like the end of the world, and most of the time it is, but in Cleveland it was deceiving. The station manager called in another bus, so the people in the front of the line left in crowded, discomfort. The overflow was less than twenty people, so we got our own seats from Cleveland to Saint Louis.

"We're going to stop in Dayton for fifteen minutes." The driver announced. "But this bus leaves in fifteen minutes, with or without you."

I had a cigarette and waited until the line at the snack bar got short, then grabbed two chicken sandwiches and a drink and rushed to the man behind the register. It picked that second to stop working. I finally told him I had to go, as he got it open to give me my change.

The nice lady in the brown dress didn't look at all flustered. She was talking to a customer. I said," The bus driver said he would leave without us."

She said, "Okay," but we left shortly after I got back without her. The mood changed, but there were twenty people on a schedule and she wanted us all to wait for her. We would have but Greyhound wouldn't. The driver even slowed to see if she would come running out, but she didn't

It didn't make any of us feel better that it was her fault. She was one of us, and she was left in Dayton, and her purse and baggage were on the bus. Someone said something about money, but it was sure she didn't leave her money on the bus.

"At least she can eat." The man with the cowboy hat said.

The real world was fun and warm in-between the anxiety and pain. It was also tragic. We talked about what we do, what we wanted to do, and how we were going to do it, as the long road grew shorter. But it wasn't the same after we left the nice lady in the brown dress in Dayton, Ohio.

#

Jesus is big in the Bible Belt. They have crosses and sculptures and billboards to let you know. I was more impressed by the unpopulated space. Queens was as overcrowded as the city once was.

The truck driver started out in Saint Louis as a guy recovering a truck for a friend. According to him, the driver had been arrested and he was sent to get it. But, ten minutes after we boarded, a girl was nice to him and the bullshit began to fly.

We were tired. The truck driver was full of energy. His was the only audible voice on the bus, so I began to hear snickers. Ten minutes later he was the owner of thirty six trucks out of seventeen states, and owned houses in all of them.

When he began telling the girl about the women who flash their tits at him over the years, the snickers turned to moans. When he began talking telling about a gal who flashed her crotch at him, the lady from Virginia reminded him there were children on the bus. Most would have shut up from embarrassment, but he began talking about Jesus, and we all wished he would go back to the pussy flashing story.

He started by telling her how much good religion could have on children and segued into the sins of homosexuality. When he started in about women's reproductive rights, the lady from Virginia reminded him again that there were children aboard, and shortly after, the black woman from Texas said, "Mister, you're offensive. Would you please shut up?"

There was no applause, but I could hear it in my head.

#

The bus out of Saint Louis was another overflow bus, so we purposely took our time and stayed at the back of the line, and had our own seats. The driver had been woken up and called in to do our run. When I told him I needed to get off in Lebanon, he laughed, and said something about someone being an idiot to his friend.

"I'll tell ya what though. Lebanon has the only food market before it becomes all vending machines until Oklahoma City. It's a little off course for us, but those machines are expensive."

Everyone loved me. Food is as important as anything when you're on the road. We stopped at a small bus depot along the way for a cigarette, then to Lebanon. It was dark and late. I stayed with my friends until the bus had to go, and then called Larry.

"Hey man, I'm here."

"I'll send you a cab. Hang out right there."

It was time to finish my story.

XVI

The first thing I noticed in Missouri was the crows. Life felt right again. After visiting a few shops, I saw the people were nice and the prices were low. I could walk to the stores from the house. The farmer's market was in town twice a week, and the town was quaint. It was perfect for what I needed.

June arrived with hot temperatures and bright skies. I stayed in the shade when I could and wrote in front of the fan when it got hot. There was a telephone, so I talked to people when I wasn't writing. Matt called to tell me that Danny was sock puppeted as a woman on Orange Papers.

When I was done laughing, I said, "Seriously, a woman?"

"They're calling him," Tranny Bennison."

"That's not nice to trannys."

"No, it's like, Trisha and Danny....Like Ben-Lo, or whatever."

"I love a good freak show, but sorry, I'm staying away from him."

Matt asked about the new book, so I explained. Then, I asked him about Doctor Gerald Davidson. "How did Davidson get to disappear the way he did?"

"I'd love to find out more about him."

"Think about it." I said. "Miler newton, Mel Sembler, Mitt Romney, Matthew Israel, all of them want the stink of their past to disappear like Davidson's. If you remember, I started that discussion because even Elan people never talked about him."

"You're not going to say he was in the CIA again, are you?"

"What else makes sense? He at least had help from some heavy hitters in the government. No one gave the go-ahead for this shit. That would have taken an act of congress. Who else but the CIA could get all those doctors to risk their careers?"

125

"Hmm."

"Yeah, hmm."

#

It was one of those things you hear a thousand times but finally hear. Linda said, "I was transferred to Waterford when Elan Seven was cleared out."

"Cleared out?"

She explained, and as she did I remembered her saying it before. It never registered until that day. According to her they transferred everyone out of Elan Seven and began taking new residents in. As Danny, the assistant resident director, said, "They began bringing in autistic kids, mentally ill, etc…"

"They left a skeleton crew of older residents—"

"I remember that. They were drug addicts. Yeah. But then they were all gone, and all that was left was killers, rapists, and nut cases."

"There you have it."

There was the question of which category I fell into. I had never been on medication or been committed, and wasn't autistic, so the news that Doctor Peck was afraid of me made me wonder if they believed me to be a sociopath, like Pat Carlson.

"I need one thing before I can say without a doubt that this was an experiment."

"What's that?"

"Something to tie Gerald Davidson and his bunch to behavior modification and autism."

I got it the next day.

#

When I wasn't writing I was reading old threads and double checking facts. I noticed his name because I couldn't remember who he was or why I posted his name on Fornits. It was enough to run a search and find his profile.

Profile

Paul E. Touchette,

Professor, Pediatrics

School of Medicine

Principal Psychologist, Child Neurology, UCI Medical Center

Ed.D., Harvard University, 1967, Psychology Research

M.Ed., Harvard University, 1963

B.A., Harvard College, 1960, Psychology

Research Interests: Behavioral Medicine, Behavior Modification in Public Health, Autism, Developmental Disabilities.

#

It was enough for me.

XVII

God came to me in a second dream and asked me to read him a story. My brother used to ask me to tell him stories when we were children—it had a familiar feel. I told God the story of my life after prison, and when I was done, he asked about my books.

"I have three written."

Though they were dreams, they felt so real. There was a blip that bothered me in the dream about the secret to happiness. It was like something you see in the corner of your eye, but I heard it with my ear. I concentrated harder until the voice became clear.

God never showed his face or figure. No shadows. The voice began to trigger a memory of a face, and the shape of his head, until there was a clear figure of a man at a desk with a pad and pen. It was Gerald Davidson.

"Who will be God?"

"Huh?" Matt asked.

"Nothing, I was thinking about that God dream again."

"The one where he turns into Davidson?"

"Yeah...Creepy."

"You can say that again."

#

Immediately after Elan closed, while we were attacking Sharon Terry, someone posted a political campaign contributor tracker website, so I ran her and Joe, and Elan and its employees. There were a number of small donations, but nothing out of the ordinary. None were the maximum contribution amount.

"That's always bugged me."

"Most of the money was under the table."

Regardless of what happened under the table, this was Joe Ricci. If he was kicking the candidate money under the table he would have made sure to have the maximum show for the public. Joe bragged about his connections, so the politicians weren't his.

"Those were Davidson's." I said. "Joe was a punk when politicians started doing favors for Elan."

"That's true."

It raised the question of how Davidson earned favor with Maine politicians. "He didn't just show up and announce that he had bribe money. He was an outsider. How did they know he could be trusted?"

"That's a good question."

I had found one last bit of evidence against Elan and Gerald Davidson which pointed to experimentation. After double checking Paul Touchette I found the 665 page brief which claimed the Seed was using treatment that was similar to Communist brainwashing.

\#

Superintendent of Documents, U.S. Government Printing Office, Washington, D.C. 20402 (Stock No. 5270-02620, $5.35)

Publication Date: 1974-11-00

Pages: 655

Pub Types: Legal/Legislative/Regulatory Materials

Abstract:

This report responds to a directive issued to the Senate Subcommittee on Constitutional Rights to conduct an investigation into behavior modification programs, with particular emphasis on the federal government's involvement in the technology of behavior control and the implications of this involvement for individual rights. Two basic considerations motivated the investigation: first, the concern that the rights of human subjects of behavioral research are sufficiently protected by adequate guidelines and review structures; and second, the question of whether the federal government has any business participating in programs that may alter the substance of individual freedom. Although the material included in this report is by no means comprehensive, some initial findings are apparent: (1) there is widespread and growing interest in the development of methods designed to predict, identify, control, and modify individual behavior; (2) few measures are being taken to resolve questions of freedom, privacy, and self-determination; (3) the Federal government is heavily involved in a variety of behavior modification programs ranging from simple reinforcement techniques to psychosurgery; and (4) a number of departments and agencies fund, participate in, or sanction research involving various aspects of behavior modification.

#

"Where do you find all this stuff?" Matt said.

"Mark taught me a few things, I learned more from there."

"Well, it's impressive. Good job with Kinney and Hyde too."

"Thanks."

We changed the subject. I told him that I had decided to stay in Missouri for a while because the cost of living was so low. My slow sales months were good enough to cover my expenses. I liked the idea of supporting myself as a writer.

"Sounds pretty cool." He said.

"Let's hope this next book is the last memoir. These things take a toll."

"I could imagine. What are you going to do next?"

"Have I told you about fan fuck?"

"No. What's that?"

"Celebrity erotica. I have a dozen of them…"

Other books by Wayne Kernochan

A Life Gone Awry: My Story of the Elan School.

Street Life: My Story

Black Dark: A Hell's Kitchen Memoir

Out of the Darkness: A Story of Love and Hate and AIDS

Quotes from Wes Fager's Blog, The Straights

"They run very close to really performing psychic murder."~ Marge Robertson, executive director of the Cincinnati Chapter of the ACLU, speaking of Straight, Inc., from Cincinnati Post

"As a proud American, I find Melvin Sembler, our ambassador to Italy, and his wife, Betty, to be profound embarrassments. It is important that their advice on the drug war and especially on drug treatment be ignored. Indeed, it might be best if Italians listened to what this powerful couple had to say about drugs - and then followed policies in precisely the opposite direction."~ Arnold Trebach, Professor Emeritus of Law at American University

"I want this girl the fuck out of my group."~Reverend Miller Newton at Straight-St Pete in Leigh Bright's face having just thrown her to the floor by her hair.

"According to sworn testimony, Straight often left restrained group members sitting in their own urine, feces or vomit until suitable concessions were extracted."~ From Treatment, Thought Reform, and the Road to Hell by Dr. Barry Beyerstein, a leading Canadian researcher on opiates and brain functioning who operates a laboratory at Simon Fraser University in British Columbia, Canada.

Quotes from Elan School's Record of Atrocities

"In late 2004, the National Institutes of Health released a "state of the science" consensus statement, concluding that "get tough" treatments "do not work and there is some evidence that they may make the problem worse." At Elan, survivors typically claim to leave with post-traumatic stress disorder and exacerbations of their original problems.""

"Don Schlosser, a spokesman for the Illinois Department of Children and Family Services, told the Associated Press that the department's evaluation team had 'never seen anything quite so bizarre and degrading.' He said 'the whole concept of this program seems to be a brain washing technique.'"

I do not recall the precise explanation for this or how the 'treatment' was supposed to help Karen. I suspect my horror outranks my memory ... but she was the first of many as we watched the student drill sergeants up close and personal in the faces of other misbehaving 'students' shrieking at the tops of their lungs: 'YOU are filth. You are nothing but filth. You are slime. You keep behaving this way and you will DIE!!!'

"As the residents surged over the scuffed linoleum of the dining room, knocking over metal chairs, Kim curled into a ball. 'You fucking bitch, fucking whore, fucking fuck-up!' Kim was enduring a 'learning experience'

"Elan did at least one thing well: it made money. With profits from the school, Mr. Ricci bought a run-down harness-racing track in Portland, Me., called Scarborough Downs. Through the years, his behavior became increasingly erratic. He gave an expletive-laced tirade against a

Maine harness-racing official over the Scarborough Downs public-address system. He was sued three times for sexual harassment, once for threatening to kill a female employee. He lost one case and settled the other two."

Death list:

Aaron Wright Bacon (16 years old), died 3/31/94 -- untreated Peritonitis

Alex Cullinane (13 years old), died 8/12/06 – under investigation

Alex Harris (12 years old) died 9/13/05 – dehydration and a blow to his head

Andrew McClain (11 years old) died 3/22/98 – traumatic asphyxiation and chest compression

Angellika 'Angie' Arndt (7 years old) died 26/05/06 – traumatic asphyxiation while restrained

Anthony Dumas (15 years old) died 6/12/00 – hanged himself. Home workers did not cut him down, took pictures, police cut him down. He died 4 months later, never coming out of his coma

Anthony Green (15 years old) died 5/21/91 -- Traumatic asphyxiation

Anthony T Haynes (14 years old) died 7/1/2001 – dehydration

Bobby Joe Randolph (17 years old) died 9/26/96 – traumatic asphyxiation

Bobby Sue Thomas (17 years old) died 8/16/96 – acute cardiac arrhythmia while restrained

Brandon Hadden (18 years old) 1998 – choked on his vomit while being restrained

Brendan Blum (14 years old) died 6/28/07 – bowel obstruction

Bryan Dale Alexander (18 years old) -- pneumonia

Caleb Jensen (15 years old) died 5/2007 – untreated severe staph infection

Cameron Hamilton (2 years old) died 12/5/05 -- severe head trauma

Candace Newmaker (10 years old) 4/18/2000 – death resulting from rebirthing

Carlton Eugene Thomas (17 years old) – restraint

Casey Collier (17 years old) 12/93 – traumatic asphyxiation

Cedric Napoleon (14 years old) 3/7/2002 – restraint

Chad Andrew Franza (16 years old) 8/17/98 – suicide by hanging

Charles "Chase" Moody Jr (17 years old) 10/14/02 – asphyxiation by restraint

Charles Collins Jr (15 years old) – forced over-exercise with known heart condition

Chloe Cohen died 2/21/? – suicide by hanging

Christopher Michael (8 years old) died 11/24/02 – abuse

Chris Campbell (13 years old) died 11/2/97 – undetermined.

Christie Scheck (13 years old) died 3/6/92 – suicide by hanging

Cindi Sohappy (16 years old) died 12/6/03 – undetermined

Corey Foster- Restraints

Corey William Murphy (17 years old) died 3/21/2000 – suicide

Daniel Matthews (17 years old) died 3/31/03 – killed by fellow inmate

Danieal Kelly (14 years old) died 8/4/06 – starvation, dehydration, cerebral palsy

Darryl Thompson (15 years old) died 10/06 – restraint

Dawn Birnbaum- Murdered after escaping the Elan School

Dawn Renay Perry (16 years old) died 4/10/93 – restraint death

Dawnne Takeuchi (18 years old) died 6/25/95 – thrown from moving vehicle

Diane Harris (17 years old) died 4/11/90 – violently restrained, asphyxiation

Dillon Taylor Peak (14 years old) died 6/17/06 – severe untreated encephalitis

Donderey Rogers died July 2002 – restraint

Dustin E Phelps (14 years old) died 3/1/98 – strapped in a blanket in bed

Earl Smith (9 years old) died 1/11/95 – asphyxiation while restrained

Edith Campos (15 years old) died 2/2/98 – restraint asphyxiation

Elisa Santry (16 years old) died 7/16/2006 – under investigation

Eddie Lee (15 years old) -- restrained, beaten

Eric Roberts (16 years old) died 2/22/96 – wrapped in plastic foam blanket

Erica Harvey (15 years old) died 5/27/2002 – hypothermia and dehydration

Faith Finley (17 years old) died 12/31/2006 – suffocated while being restrained

Gareth Myatt (15 years old) died 4/04 – restraint

Garrett Halsey (16 years old) died 12/23/04 – autistic and mentally retarded, restraint death

Gina Score (14 years old) died 1990 – hyperthermia

Ian August (14 years old) died 7/13/2002 – hyperthermia

Isaiah Simmons died 1/23/2007 – restrained

Jamal Odum (9 years old) – restraint death

Jamar Griffiths (15 years old) died 10/18/94 – traumatic asphyxiation

James White (17 years old) died 12/05

Jamie Young (13 years old) died 6/5/93 – heatstroke and dehydration with overdose of antidepressants

Jason Tallman (12 years old) died 5/12/93 – suffocated while restrained

Jeffrey Bogrett (9 years old) died 12/1/95 – restraint

Jeffry Demetrius (17 years old) died 9/26/97 – strangulation while being restrained

Jerry Mclaurin (14 years old) died 11/2/99 – restraint

Jimmy Kanda (6 years old) died 9/20/97-- strangulation while restrained in wheelchair

Jimmy Shiplett- Killed by Ken Zaretsky at the Elan School.

Joey (Giovanni) Alteriz (16 years old) died 2/4/06 – asphyxiation while restrained

John McCloskey (18 years old) died 2/24/96 – ruptured colon, torn liver, torn small intestine from being sodomized with a broom-like handle

Johnny Lim (14 years old) died 12/26/05 spontaneous brain-stem hemorrhage

Jonathan Carey (13 years old) died 2/15/07 – asphyxiation while restrained in van

Joshua Ferarini (13 years old) died 1/8/89 – suffocation while restrained

Joshua Sharpe (17 years old) died 12/28/99 – restraint

Karlye Newman (16 years old) died 10/8/2004 – suicide by hanging

Kasey Warner (13 years old) died 10/8/2005 – drowning

Katherine Lank (16 years old) died 1/13/2002 – massive head trauma

Katherine Rice (16 years old) died 5/2/2008 – overdose of methadone

Kelly Young (17 years old) died 3/4/98 – position asphyxiation while restrained

Keyana Bravo-Hamilton (2 years old) died 9/4/06 – abuse, internal injuries

Kerry Layne Brown (24 years old) died 6/6/06 –

Kristal Mayon-Ceniceros (16 years old) died 2/5/99 – respiratory arrest from restraint

Kristen Chase (16 years old) died 6/27/90 – heatstroke

Kyle Young (16 years old) – pushed by guards into elevator doors that opened, he fell down the shaft

LaKeisha Brown (17 years old) died 4/9/2005 – medical neglect

Latasha Bush (15 years old) died 2/14/2002 – restraint asphyxiation

Lenny Ortega (12 years old) died 5/31/2002 – drowned

Linda Harris (14 years old) died 9/18/2005 – asphyxiation while restrained

Leroy Prinkley (14 years old) died 9/28/88 cerebral anoxia from forceful restraint

Maria Mendoza (14 years old) died 10/12/2003 – traumatic asphyxiation while restrained

Marcus Fiesel (3 years old) died Aug 2006 – taped into high chair, left for two days, then his body burned. Cause of death unknown

Mario Cano (16 years old) – blood clot

Mark Draheim (14 years old) died 12/98 – asphyxiation while restrained

Matthew Goodman (14years old) died 2/6/2002 – pneumonia, respiratory distress and blood poisoning from being kept in mechanical restraints for 16 months

Mark Soares (16 years old) died 4/29/98 cardiac arrest from physical restraint

Martin Lee Anderson (14 years old) died 1/6/2006 – asphyxiation from ammonia capsules being shoved up his nose

Melissa Neyman (19 years old) died 7/24/97 – hanged in restraint straps

Michael Arnold (19 years old) died 7/15/97 asphyxiation while restrained

Michael (Christening) Carcia (12 years old) died 12/2005 – restraint

Michael IbarraWiltsie (12 years old) died 2/5/2000 -- asphyxiation while restrained

Michael Lewis III, (15 years old) died 8/25/2003 – restraint

Natalynndria Lucy Slim (16 years old) died 7/13/06) -- suicide by hanging

Nicholas Contreras (16 years old) died 3//98 – prolonged serious medical neglect

Omar Paisley (17 years old) died 6/9/2003 – untreated ruptured appendix

Omega Leach (17 years old) died June 2007 – restraint

Orlena Parker (15 years old) died 3/10/2003 – restraint

Paul Choy (16 years old) died 1992 – restraint

Phil Williams- Beaten to death my residents on orders from staff at the Elan School

Raijon Daniels (8 years old) died 10/26/06 – prolonged intense abuse

Randy Steele (9 years old) died 2/6/2000 – suffocation while restrained

Robert Doyle Erwin (15 years old) – drowning

Robert Rollins (12 years old) died 4/21/97 – asphyxiation while restrained

Roberto Reyes (15 years old) died 11/3/04 – rhabdomyolysis

Rochelle Clayborne (16 years old) died 8/18/97 – cardiac arrhythmia after receiving tranquilizers

Roxanna Gray (17 years old) died 7/6/89 – suffocation while restrained

Ryan Lewis (14 years old) died 2/13/2001 – suicide by hanging

Sabrina E Day (15 years old) died 2/10/2000 – restraint

Sakena Dorsey (18 years old) died 6/10/97 – suffocation while restrained, history of asthma

Sarah Crider (14 years old) died 2/13/06 – intestinal blockage, bacterial sepsis, vomit in her lungs, infection of the bloodstream

Sergey Blashchishena (16 years old) died 8/28/2009 – cause of death unknown

Shinaul McGraw (12 years old) died 6/5/97 – hyperthermia, wrapped in sheet and restrained with gauze over his mouth

Shawn Smith (13 years old) died 10/30/2001 – suicide by hanging

Shirley Arciszewski (12 years old) died 09/05 -- restraint death, asphyxia

Stephanie Duffield (16 years old) died 2/11/01 – restraint

Stephen Komminos (22 years old) died 10/04/07 – choking

Timothy Thomas (9 years old) – restraint death

Tanner Wilson (11 years old) died 2/9/01 – heart attack while restrained

Anthony 'Tony' Haynes (14 years old) -- Heat exhaustion, suspected abuse

Thomas Mapes (17 years old) died 7/8/94 – asphyxiation while handcuffed

Travis Parker (13 years old) died 4/21/05 – denied asthma medication while restrained

Tristan Sovern (16 years old) died 3/4/98 – asphyxiation while restrained

Unnamed (16 years old) died 7/2/2004 – suicide by hanging

Unidentified (16 years old) died April 2007 – suicide by hanging

Valerie Ann Heron (17 years old) died 8/10/2001 – suicide by jumping from balcony

Victoria Petersilka died 2/9/02 – suicide by hanging

Walter Brown (18 years old) died Jan 2005 – restrained

Wauketta Wallace (12 years old) died 7/11/89 – postural asphyxiation from restraint

Will Futrelle (15 years old) died 3/25/96 – murdered by other students

William (Eddie) Lee (15 years old) died 9/18/2000 – injury at base of skull from being restrained

Willie Lawrence Durden III (17years old) died 10/14/2003 – untreated ventricular arrhythmia

Willie Wright (9 years old) died 2/4/2000 – restraint

Bernard Reefer died 11/24/80

Carlos Ruiz (13 years old) died 12/16/94

Carter Lynn died 6/7/06 – suicide by hanging

Carles Lucas (16 years old) died 11/24/80 – drowning

Christopher Brown (16 years old) died 3/26/03 – hit by train while running away

Corey Baines (16 years old) died 3/26/03 – tree fell on tent while sleeping

Danny Lewis (16 years old) died 6/89

Eric David Schibley (17 years old) died 11/24/80 – drowning

James Lamb (14 years old) died 11/24/80 – drowning

John Avila died 7/25/94

John Vincent Garrison (18 years old)

Kristen Chase (16 years old) died 6/27/90

Laura Hanson (17 years old) died 11/19/98

Leon Anger died 9/16/84

Lorenzo Johnson (17 years old) died 6/27/94 – drowned while running away

Lyle Foodroy – drowned

ML – shot and killed himself

Matt Toppi (17 years old) died 3/7/98 -- hit by train while running away

143

RC died 4/10/05 -- suicide

Robert Zimmerman (17 years old) died 11/24/80 – drowning

Rocco Magliozzi (12 years old) died 7/28/06 – West Nile Virus and Rocky Mountain Spotted Fever

Tammy Edmiston died 9/11/82

All these children died while in care or as a result of care in residential treatment facilities, boot camps, wilderness programs, behavior modification programs, and other private and state sponsored facilities.

Made in the USA
Middletown, DE
09 April 2021